WOODLAND WORKSHOP

WOODLAND
WORKSHOP

TOOLS AND DEVICES
FOR WOODLAND CRAFT

BEN LAW

First published 2018 by
Guild of Master Craftsman Publications Ltd
Castle Place, 166 High Street, Lewes,
East Sussex BN7 1XU

Reprinted 2019

Text © Ben Law, 2018
Copyright in the Work © GMC Publications Ltd,
2018

ISBN 978 1 78494 343 1

Publisher Jonathan Bailey
Production Jim Bulley, Jo Pallet
Senior Project Editor Virginia Brehaut
Editor Robin Pridy
Managing Art Editor Gilda Pacitti
Art Editor Rebecca Mothersole
Photographer Andrew Perris
Illustrator Jane Bottomley
Cover illustration Celia Hart

Colour origination by GMC Reprographics
Printed and bound in China

CONTENTS

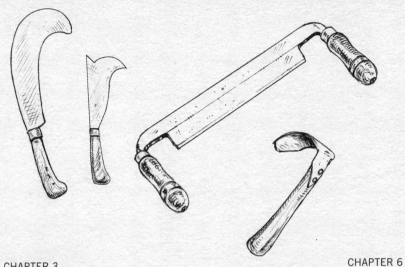

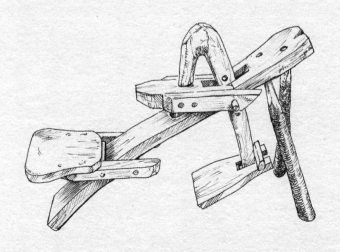

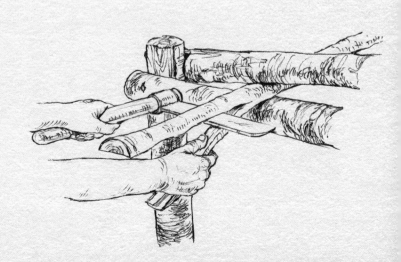

Introduction

Diverse and useful devices have formed and shaped the heritage of the woodland crafts we have today. Made from the coppice woodlands that also supply the craft materials, in conjunction with the traditional range of green woodworking tools, this amalgamation forms the woodland workshop.

Often referred to as 'another pair of hands', these devices have originated from individual craftspeople who have needed to grip or clamp or hold a piece of wood. They have, over time, evolved into the patterns I have described here. Some remain almost unchanged from early designs, while others have been adapted to the needs of different crafts and some are new designs ready to help out with the making of more modern woodland crafts.

For anyone embarking upon the pleasure of working with greenwood, these projects should be amongst the first you undertake. Without some of these devices, making your craft produce from coppiced poles will be challenging. A cleaving brake will help ensure the even splitting of the pole into smaller dimensions, and a knee vice or shaving horse will grip your cleft material while you draw knife the material down to your chosen dimension.

Although it is possible to purchase the more common designs, making your own will not only give you the satisfaction and pride that comes from transforming the raw material of coppiced wood into your own unique device but will be a good learning process and help to build up your confidence working with greenwood edge tools. They will also be ergonomically suited to you, helping to ensure you look after your body as you make your craft.

These projects are based on designs old and new, all of which have their place in the woodland workshop, be it under a tarpaulin in the coppice while making chestnut pales or under the solid roof of a permanent workshop. They are all adaptable and indeed should be adapted to make them ergonomic for the user and specialized for the particular craft.

The evolution of the shaving horse is now unfolding and growing in many directions, producing unique designs, and this year I have enjoyed adapting the Sussex knee vice to take a pivot peg and am considering further evolution as the device becomes more integral to the craft produce I make. For me, the yogic position of the full stretch of the body on a knee vice can be a pleasant change from many hours sat upon a shaving horse.

Above all, I hope this book brings inspiration to a new generation of craftspeople to take knowledge from the ideas of the past, restore some of the many derelict coppice woodlands to their productive glory and make the craft produce of the future.

OPPOSITE PAGE: Using a workshop chopping block to shape a billet with a side axe.

ABOVE RIGHT: Using a ladder knee vice to peel a pole.

LEFT: Using the Sussex knee vice
(see page 74) to peel a pole with a draw knife.

ABOVE: The shaving horse 2000 developed
by Mike Abbott (see page 124).

BELOW LEFT: Honing a chisel with a leather
strop (see page 54).

BELOW CENTRE (UPPER): A butterpat joint
created with gouges and framing chisels used
in roundwood timber framing (see page 37).

BELOW CENTRE (LOWER): Chestnut laths
in a bundling device (see page 172).

BELOW RIGHT: Peeling a pole with a draw
knife on the shaving horse 2000 (see page 124).

ABOVE LEFT: Laloosh, the workshop cat.

ABOVE RIGHT: Apprentices Andy French and Ben Austin preparing trellis poles in the workshop at Prickly Nut Wood.

LEFT: Chestnut shakes made with a shake brake (see page 134), bundled and ready to despatch.

RIGHT: Cleaving a chestnut rod with a Sussex adze (see page 34).

BELOW LEFT: A bucket full of pegs and peg blanks for roundwood timber framing.

BELOW RIGHT: Using a triangulated cleaving brake (see page 146) to cleave a chestnut rod.

THE WORKSHOP

'A PLACE OF SHELTER WHERE ONE CAN CARRY OUT WOODLAND CRAFT.'

A woodland workshop can take many forms, from a simple tarpaulin stretched across a wooden pole, to a solid built and well-organized building. Workshops are the heart space of the craftsperson, and a well-organized workshop will bring feelings of immense pleasure as you enter the space to begin your day's work.

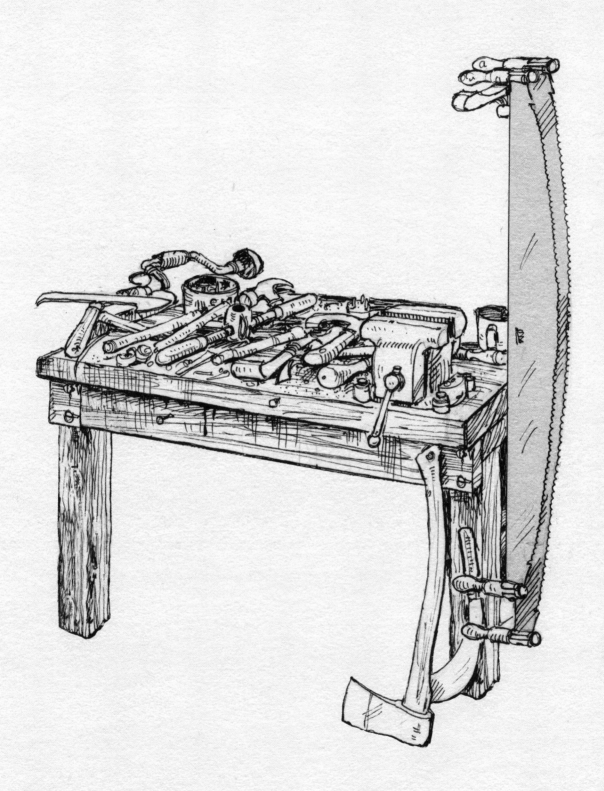

TEMPORARY WORKSHOPS

A workshop should provide reasonable shelter from the elements,
the tools and devices necessary to carry out the woodland task,
and a stove/fire for boiling a kettle. It also needs to have good
natural light for carrying out specific crafts.

Uses of temporary workshops

I have worked with a number of temporary workshops, built deep in the woods. They have served me well while I convert a particular cant (area) of coppice to its finished product. Cutting coppice in the winter will vary year to year – using a temporary workshop when the rain lashes down allows productivity to continue and keeps you dry but out in the winter air.

For a lot of chestnut craft produce such as pale making and lath making, it is often more efficient to convert the coppiced timber to the finished product in a temporary workshop in the woodland than to transport hundreds of 4–8in (100–200mm) poles back to a solid workshop and yard. By converting to the finished product within the woodland, only the finished product itself needs to be extracted and delivered.

Placement

For a simple temporary workshop, I choose a spot where there are a couple of suitable standard trees that will support a pole suspended between them. The pole becomes a ridge pole for a large tarpaulin that is pegged to the ground or lashed to suitable stumps with guy ropes. To stretch out the edges of the tarpaulin, I attach a thinner pole, threaded through webbing loops sewn to the tarpaulin and use progs (forked sticks) to adjust the tension and angle of each side of the tarpaulin.

Temporary workshop in chestnut coppice for pale making.

What to include

For pale making, my temporary workshop contained a cleaving brake, peeling jig, chopping block and a rocket stove for boiling the kettle. This stove is a very simple and efficient way of boiling water in a temporary workshop and needs only a little wood to achieve a good boil.

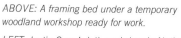

ABOVE: A framing bed under a temporary woodland workshop ready for work.

LEFT: Justin Owen's lath workshop in National Trust woods near Haslemere, Surrey, UK.

RIGHT: Rocket stove boiling a kettle.

Designing your temporary workshop

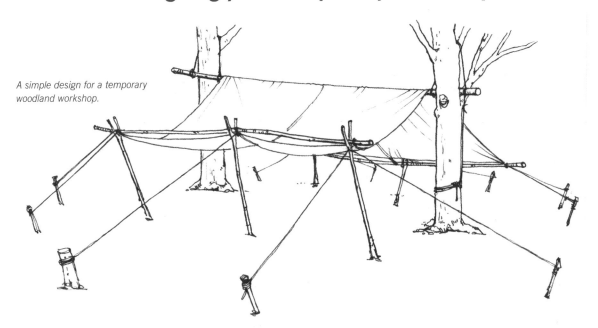

A simple design for a temporary woodland workshop.

Many designs of temporary workshop can be found amongst those working in the woods. The important things to consider are:

How windy is the site?
Temporary structures and high winds are not a good combination!

How large a workshop do you need?
What must it shelter and how many of you are using the workshop?

How long is the workshop to be used for?
If it is for just a few weeks, the design will be very simple, if it is for a few months, you should allow more time for construction.

Position within the woodland
It is best to position your workshop as near as possible to the access point in the wood, as all finished produce will be extracted that way.

TOP RIGHT: Inside the temporary workshop, there is plenty of space for carrying out the craft.

RIGHT: Mike Abbott's Brookfield Wood workshop, designed for a season of greenwood working courses. Here, it is being used for bow making.

SOLID WORKSHOPS

A solid workshop, where your tools are well organized and
easy to find, where projects can be left until the next day with
the knowledge that no one will move them is, to many
craftworkers, the ultimate goal. I, too, look forward to
one day enjoying this paradise.

The workshop at Prickly Nut Wood.

Leaving tools and work on the workbench can only be done when working on your own.

Sharing a space

Although I have a solid workshop, I share my workshop with my apprentices and a shared workshop is a different venue to a personal workshop. Sharing a workshop relies upon trust, understanding and clear rules of what is expected from all the users. Projects cannot be left half finished on the workbench, and tools need to be put back in their correct place, having been sharpened ready for the next user. Occasionally, between apprentices, I regain the workshop for myself and enjoy the indulgence of leaving projects on the workbench ready to start again the next day.

Seasonal changes

As a coppice worker, my workshop has to be flexible throughout the year as different seasons bring different uses for the space. In the winter, the workshop is primarily a forester's workshop, with chainsaw maintenance, sharpening and filling of chainsaw bars a daily occurrence. Wedges, winches, strops and shackles are on hand for regular use, as are felling levers and timber tongs. At the end of each day, this collection of tools is returned to the workshop as the daylight disappears.

As spring approaches, the forestry equipment takes a back-seat role in the workshop with many items stored away until the next cutting season. Spring brings a change of season both in the woods and in my workshop. Spring brings the craft season, the adding of value to the coppiced wood that was felled during the winter. Different items will need to be made: some individual projects, others bulk orders for which the workshop may need to be adapted.

Special projects

On a recent large 'shake' order, I set up three temporary workstations with soft-jawed vices to enable maximum productivity and best use of the workshop space. After the completion of the order these workstations were dismantled, leaving the workshop open and ready for the next projects.

Workshop adapted for shake making and ready for a sweep-up after a day's work.

Important considerations for a solid workshop

Planning permission?

A permanent building will need planning permission. A workshop used as a forestry building will have permitted development rights but prior notification to your local planning authority will be needed.

What size?

Design the workshop's size to allow space for the crafts you plan to carry out. Consider doorway sizes – your finished product may be much larger than the pieces of wood brought into the workshop to make it!

Light/power?

Do you need electricity for lights/power tools or are you going to work purely with hand tools and natural light? Roof windows considerably aid natural light.

Materials?

Where are you building the workshop? What materials are available and how well will it blend into its natural environment? A well-designed building that sits quietly in its surroundings is likely to be looked upon more favourably by your local planning department.

Access?

The workshop will need reasonable access for bringing in wood and taking out products to sell.

Using natural light available in the workshop to make chestnut shakes.

My workshop at Prickly Nut Wood

Nestled within the woodland, my workshop needed to be designed to sit gently in its sylvan landscape. I designed the building from materials I had around me.

I chose to build using roundwood timber framing techniques, as this is my speciality and I had a suitable selection of chestnut and larch poles growing in the woodland to use. I went for large barn doors at each end for getting large projects in and out. I made the floor from oak I felled and milled and it has proved hard-wearing and good for adaptation as I fit temporary work stations or secure timber to it, to aid products I am making.

Roofing

The roof is a 45-degree pitch with a 'cat slide' that creates an outside area for seasoning timber. I chose a 45-degree pitch with the aim that one day I will make shakes for the roof to match my house. For the current time, I have used green corrugated roofing sheets, made from plant fibre and bitumen. These are quick to put up and blend in pretty well in a rural setting.

Power source

The south-facing side of the roof is fitted with photovoltaic panels (PVs), for solar electricity. My workshop, like my house, is 'off grid', but with good battery storage and an inverter, I can run power tools and table saws up to 2,500 watts. This makes me work well in tune with the weather – if I have a need for machining timber, I choose a sunny day! The roof also feeds into a 10,000-litre (2,640-US gallon) underground rainwater storage tank, which ensures I have enough water for steam bending, and provides summer irrigation for my vegetable garden. I have an old woodburner but I am considering upgrading to a workshop stove that will burn sawdust as well as logs and timber offcuts. The design I am looking into has a unique double air tube for sawdust burning that ensures you turn all your waste into warming your workplace.

ABOVE RIGHT: The workshop under construction – notice the temporary workshop set up to aid construction.

CENTRE RIGHT: The workshop roof with solar PV panels.

RIGHT: Example of an Oakfire workshop stove for sawdust and timber burning.

Shaping a peg blank on a Dumbhead shaving horse in my workshop at Prickly Nut Wood.

THE KEY TOOLS FOR WOODLAND CRAFT

There are a number of tools that have traditionally been used for green woodworking. Some have been partially superseded by power-based alternatives, but the majority are in regular use and form the basis of the green woodworker's toolkit. Many tools are handmade and unique, often adapted to the user. Tools made by larger tool manufacturers are more common – it is a personal choice which you choose.

Draw knife

It is a rare project that starts with a log, ends up as a finished craft piece and does not involve a draw knife. The name comes from the process of drawing the knife towards you as you shape or reduce the size of a piece of greenwood.

Construction

A draw knife consists of a blade, usually with a single bevel and two wooden handles that are fitted over the tangs (projected parts of the knife). The angle of the handles will affect the use of the knife. Many draw knives have the handles cranked downwards and splayed out a little. This allows for the knife to be used bevel side up or down and I find this a more ergonomic tool than draw knives with handles level to the blade. However, choice of knife and design is very personal to the user and the craft they are pursuing.

Blade

The size of the blade can vary on a draw knife from about 4–16in (100–400mm), and I have different-sized draw knives for different uses. The smaller-bladed draw knives I use for more detailed work – for example, for removing excess wood off a chair leg before finishing with a spoke shave. Larger-bladed knives are often used for peeling bark and I use a draw knife to finish large timbers that I am using for roundwood timber framing.

Selection of draw knives in the workshop.

Finish

The finish on the poles from a draw knife is not perfect but shows the hand work of the craftsperson. For most green woodworkers the draw knife is used with a shaving horse to hold the wood, while the operator is seated on the horse, drawing the knife towards themselves.

Viking beginnings

The State Historical Museum in Stockholm, Sweden, has reference to the use of a draw knife in Viking shipwright's tools around AD 1000.

Peeling a pole with a draw knife, using a shaving horse 2000.

Spoke shave

The spoke shave is a two-handled tool with a small blade, usually 2–4in (50–100mm) in length. The tool has its origins in the draw knife but is a more refined tool. With its cutting depth restricted, it gives the craftsperson greater control. The name comes from its use by wheelwrights, who needed to evenly finish the spokes on the wheels they were making.

Uses

In many respects the spoke shave is a small plane that can be used to follow curves, as in a chair leg or tool handle. It can be pushed or pulled and is often used after a draw knife (see page 26) or adze (see page 34) to give a finer finish to the project you are working on.

Construction

Traditional spoke shaves were wooden-handled, but modern spoke shaves are usually of metal construction and have easily removable blades for sharpening. Convex and concave designs are available for specific tasks.

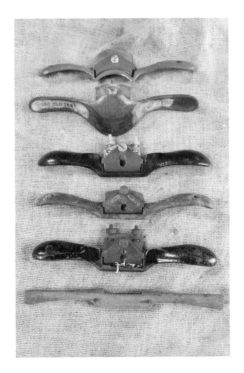

OPPOSITE PAGE: Finishing a chair leg with a spoke shave.

FAR LEFT: Selection of spoke shaves, including convex and concave blades.

LEFT: The legs and arms of this ladder-back chair have been finished with a spoke shave.

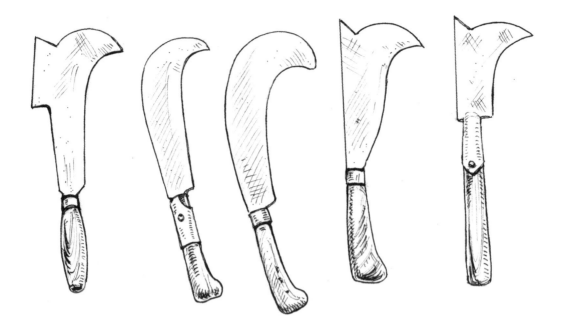

Billhook

The billhook or handbill is the traditional 'go to' tool of the countryside. There are hundreds of different pattern designs for billhooks with regional variations and different uses. The names of Elwell, Fussells, Brades, Nash, Harrison, Gilpin and Moss will make most coppice workers salivate to get their hands on the tool.

Construction

Today, Morris of Dunsford and a few individual blacksmiths carry the tradition of what was once the vast industry of billhook makers. The billhook blade is attached to the wooden handle by a tang that is part of the forged tool. This runs through the handle and is hammered over where it appears out of the end of the handle. This tang gives the tool its strength.

OPPOSITE PAGE: Snedding a sweet chestnut yurt pole with a 'Devon pattern' billhook.

Using the billhook

I use a billhook primarily for snedding coppiced poles, both chestnut (*Castanea sativa*) and hazel (*Corylus avellana*), occasional cleaving of hazel (although my preference is to use the Sussex adze), and hedge laying. From October to the end of March, rarely a day goes by in Prickly Nut Wood when a billhook is not in use. The billhook is the coppicer's tool and most coppice workers who make their craft in the woods – like hurdle makers – will have different billhooks for different stages of their craft. The billhook is the first tool of use, for felling short rotation coppice and then snedding the poles prior to making the craft.

Ancient origins

The earliest billhooks date back to 3,000 years ago in Ancient Egypt, where they were found cast in bronze. Examples of pre-Roman billhooks have been found in England and the tool has been in constant use ever since.

A twybil is shown here lying on the bed of a shaving horse. It is important that the knife end is kept very sharp.

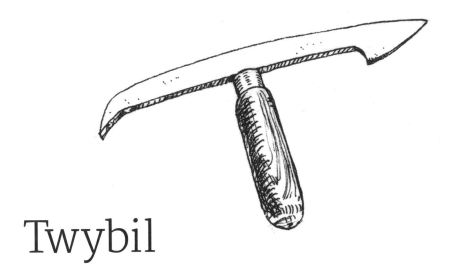

Twybil

A twybil or morticing knife is not a very commonly used tool. It was designed for cutting out the surplus wood between two or more drilled holes to form a mortice.

Shape and use

The tool is 'T'-shaped with a central handle and the steel part of the tool has at one end a sharp cutting knife and at the other a hook for cleaning out the waste, which resembles the 'ferret' often used for cleaning out the mortice slots in ladder-back chairs. The cutting job can be carried out with a chisel but if you are making a lot of mortices, the purchase of a twybil will soon pay for itself. I make a lot of chestnut gate hurdles and these have oval mortices. The curved ends are formed by part of the drilled hole and then the middle section is cut out along the grain with the twybil.

BELOW LEFT: Using the twybil to cut out an oval mortice in a gate hurdle.

BELOW: Completed chestnut gate hurdle.

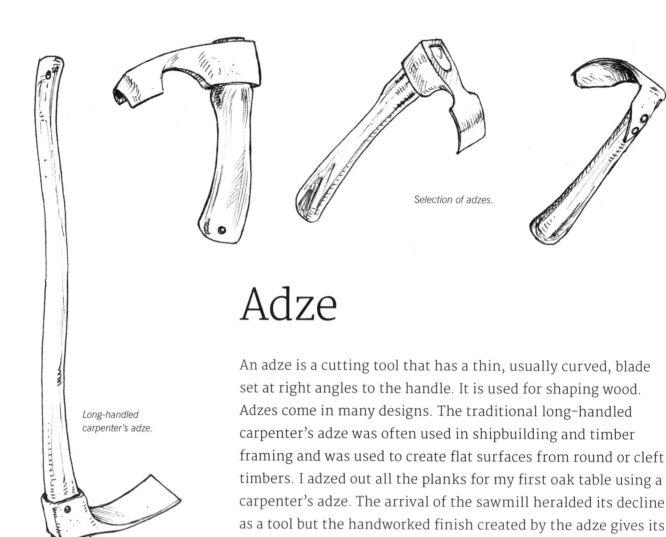

Selection of adzes.

Long-handled carpenter's adze.

Adze

An adze is a cutting tool that has a thin, usually curved, blade set at right angles to the handle. It is used for shaping wood. Adzes come in many designs. The traditional long-handled carpenter's adze was often used in shipbuilding and timber framing and was used to create flat surfaces from round or cleft timbers. I adzed out all the planks for my first oak table using a carpenter's adze. The arrival of the sawmill heralded its decline as a tool but the handworked finish created by the adze gives its products a unique look and feel.

The ancient adze

The earliest adzes were likely made from reindeer antlers in the Stone Age but civilizations around the world have used adzes for thousands of years. Ancient Egyptian art from around 2,000 BC depicts craftsmen using a tool of similar design with blades made of stone.

Types of adze

Green woodworkers regularly use hand adzes. These fall into two main categories: the curved hollowing adze with a shorter handle and curved blade that is used for hollowing bowls, troughs and chair seats; and the straighter blade of the cleaving adze that is used for riving small diameter wood. The 'Sussex adze' is a small adze used primarily for cleaving hazel or chestnut rods of about 1in (25mm) diameter.

Cleaving a chestnut rod with a Sussex adze.

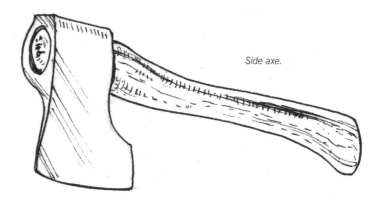

Side axe.

Axe

There is a multitude of different designs of axe. The axe has two main actions in its use: cutting and splitting. The edge must be sharp enough to cut the wood and then the shape of the head behind follows the initial cut and opens up the wood.

Blacksmith-made side axe resting in the workshop chopping block.

Use

I use long-handled splitting axes for firewood and smaller hand-held axes for carving and shaping greenwood prior to draw knifing down to a finished product. The axe I use the most in green woodworking is the side axe. This axe is bevelled on only one side and left- and right-handed versions are available.

The side axe is particularly useful for creating a straight edge from a round or cleft piece of timber. I find a light side axe the perfect tool for cutting straight edges on chestnut roofing shakes.

From stone to blade

Over 8,000 years ago, early hand axes – sharp-edged stones without handles – were used as a weapon as well as a tool for splitting, and for skinning animals. These stone heads were eventually attached to a wooden shaft and the natural progression of the blade, through copper, bronze and then steel, left us with the tool we know today.

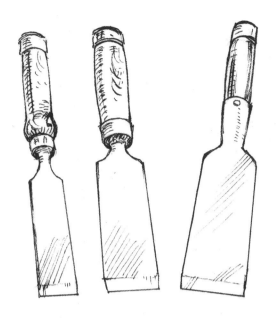

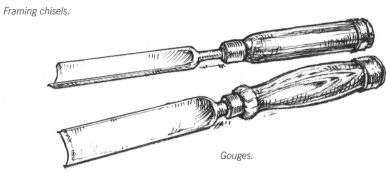

Framing chisels.

Gouges.

Chisel

The chisel is a long-bladed hand tool with a bevelled cutting edge. It has a wooden handle that is struck with a maul, mallet or hammer to cut into the wood. There are many different types that have been designed for particular uses. I have focused on the main types that I use for green woodworking and timber framing.

Main types
Chisels come in many forms but the main chisels I use are:

Framing chisel
These heavy duty long-handle chisels are used for timber framing and are struck with a maul. They have a steel hoop around the top of the handle to absorb regular blows.

Slick
The slick is really a chisel/plane with a long handle. It is used without a maul for planing a finish or creating a taper. Used traditionally in boat building, it is enjoying a renaissance in timber framing.

RIGHT: A selection of framing chisels.
FAR RIGHT: A slick.

OPPOSITE PAGE:
A selection of chisels
in the workshop.

LEFT: Framing gouges.

ABOVE: A butterpat joint created with gouges and framing chisels, used in roundwood timber framing.

Gouges

Used for carving, gouge chisels are gently struck with a maul. Framing gouges are a heavier duty tool with a steel hoop around the top of the handle to take heavier blows. I use framing gouges for carving out the butterpat joints we use in roundwood timber framing.

Corner chisels

Particularly useful when cutting a mortice, these 'L'-shaped right-angle chisels are struck with a maul.

A corner chisel being used to cut a mortice.

A very English chisel

Steel chisel production in England has its traditional heart in Sheffield's water-wheel powered factories. Robert Sorby, a company that began in 1837, is still producing fine chisels there today. I have modern Sorby chisels and other Sorby chisels that date back over 100 years; all are in regular use. Modern artisan chisels can also be obtained from the growing number of small-scale hand-forged toolmakers.

Cross-cutting a chestnut pole with a Japanese saw.

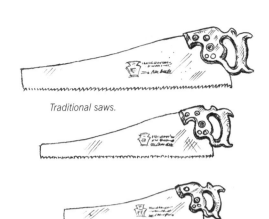
Traditional saws.

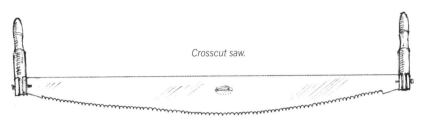
Crosscut saw.

Saw

There are panel saws for crosscutting, rip saws for sawing down the grain, and tenon and dovetail saws for specific jointing techniques. I also use the chainsaw, which, when in the right hands, is an essential tool for productive woodland management.

British vs Japanese way

Through much of the world, saws were designed to cut on the push stroke. This led to many problems with buckling blades in early saws. The Japanese set and sharpened their saws to cut on the pull stroke, a wisdom we are now reaping the benefits of in the Western world as we appreciate the craftwork and cutting ability of these tools.

Production

Today, the majority of traditional saws have been replaced by mass-produced disposable ones designed not to be re-sharpened. Yet wooden-handled saws are still produced and, with the correct sharpening files and saw-setting tools for adjusting the teeth, one saw can last a lifetime.

Pit sawing.

Saw 'dogs'

Early saws were used in a pit and it required two people: one was the person sawing above (the 'top dog') and the other would saw below (the 'underdog'). There are the remnants of an old pit in the woods where I work and the cant (the area of coppice woodland) there is known as 'sawpit piece'.

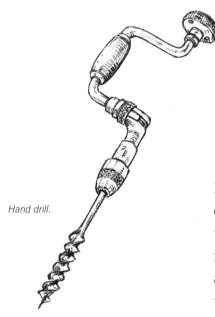

Hand drill.

Drill

It seems we have been rotating one material on top of another to carve out a hollow since our earliest days. A stick rubbed between the palms of your hands creates friction and that in turn creates fire. The next quantum leap was the bow drill. By attaching a cord around the stick and the ends of the cord to a longer bowed stick, the rate of friction could be increased.

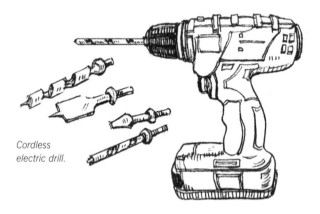

Cordless electric drill.

Going electric

Over time we have developed a range of drilling implements, many of which, such as the auger and the brace and bit, still have a place in my workshop, but the innovation of the cordless electric drill has made many older tools redundant. I am a great fan of the cordless drill. I remember making my first yurt and using a hand drill and bit to drill 700 holes through the trellis poles – a slow and tedious job with a hand drill but quick and rewarding with a cordless drill. As I most regularly work with chestnut, pre-drilling before adding any fixing is a standard requirement, so the cordless drill is most welcome in my workshop.

Japanese WoodOwl bits, my choice of modern auger.

Hand drill use

Bar or Scotch-eyed augers can be useful when making crafts out in the woods as they require no electricity. I have a 1¾in (44.5mm) auger that is great for drilling mortice holes for legs in rustic furniture – the slow and controlled action is more suitable for this type of work than the fast pace of an electric drill with a 1¾in (44.5mm) auger bit.

Auger bits

There is a wide selection of modern auger bits available to be used with electric drills. I have had a lot of experience using different patterns as I drill a very large number of holes for pegs when I am timber framing. One auger stands out above the others and that is the Japanese pattern WoodOwl bits. These never get stuck, they remove all waste and leave the inside of the hole looking like it has been polished.

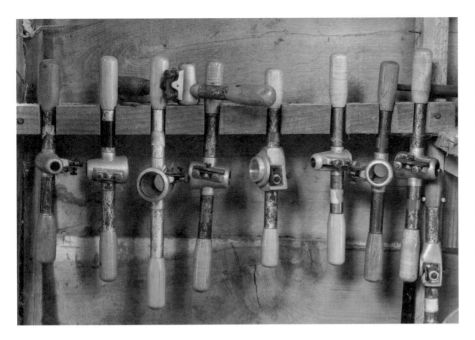
A collection of rounding planes in my workshop.

Using a rounding plane to create a 1in (25mm) peg.

Rounding Plane

Rounding or rotary planes are usually made from an aluminium casting and resemble a giant pencil sharpener with a spoke shave fitted for the blade. Each plane is cast to a fixed size so that the exit point will be, for example, 1in (25mm) and the entry point larger. With a wooden handle on each side of the casting, the plane is turned and a dowel of exactly 1in (25mm) is created.

Adding speed

Mechanized turning heads can speed up the process whereby the wood is clamped by a collet and rotated by a motor and the rounding plane is gently eased along the wood while the turning head does the work. I have a turning head made from a 120-volt motor with a Reliant Robin gearbox (constructed for me by Peter Hindle of Ashem Crafts). I use this primarily for creating pegs for roundwood timber framing and it is a fast way to produce 100 accurately sized pegs.

Use

Rounding planes are commonly used for chair making and early planes were used for making ladder rungs for apple picking ladders. Rounding planes are more versatile than the excellent tenon cutters that are available to be used with a cordless drill, as the rounding plane can produce long lengths of dowel rather than just a short length for a tenon. I have eight rounding planes. They are regularly used in many different projects and are a core part of my workshop toolkit.

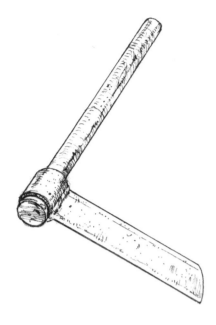

Froe

The Froe (also called a 'dill-axe' in Kent) is an 'L'-shaped tool used for cleaving or riving wood. It consists of a metal blade and usually a wooden handle. The length of the blade determines the diameter of the wood you can split, and the length of the handle the amount of leverage that can be exerted to help prise the fibres of wood apart.

Uses

The froe splits wood in a similar way to an axe but the froe can be positioned in the exact position that you wish the split to run and can split far longer pieces of wood than an axe. I split 180in (4572mm) lengths of chestnut when I am preparing timber to create yurt hoops. The froe is used in conjunction with a cleaving brake to help control and, if necessary, change the direction of the cleave.

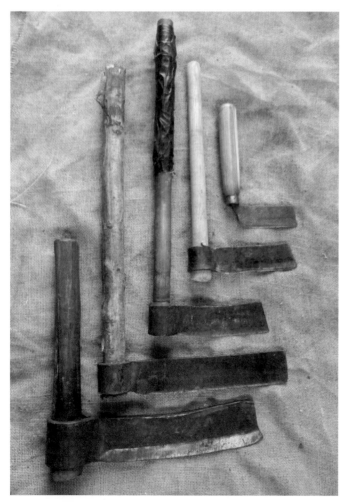

Selection of froes with micro-froe at the top and shake froe at the bottom. The froe in the centre is my favourite general-purpose cleaving froe.

Size

I have different froes for different uses. My large froes are shake froes, used for cleaving out shakes from wood up to 14in (356mm) diameter. My smallest froe is a micro-froe used for cleaving out small rods of hazel or chestnut. The next smallest are lath froes, used for the more delicate control of splitting laths from chestnut.

My favourite froe

Everyone has favourite tools – it is hard to explain the connection and feeling that runs from the body, through your hands to the tool and back again. When it is right you just know it, and no other similar tool can replicate that connection. My favourite froe is a medium-sized one that I use for a wide range of crafts from pales to split palisades. I have welded a cranked metal handle – made from a piece of old water pipe – onto this, which gives a good balance and extra leverage.

Using a froe to cleave out chestnut for gate hurdle rails.

SHARPENING

Sharpening is an essential skill that every woodworker needs to learn. There are many different opinions about the best methods and choice of tools to use for sharpening. What I will share with you here are the techniques and sharpening methods that work for me as well as the tools I use.

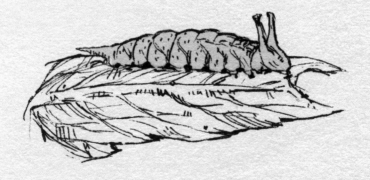

Sharpening tools for woodland crafts

The techniques and tools for sharpening are many and, for a novice woodworker, the array of available products to purchase can be daunting.

Duller vs sharper

Different tools require different sharpening techniques and some need a duller edge than others. It is by choice that the majority (lath froe an exception) of my cleaving froes do not have a very sharp edge. Their job is to prise the fibres of the wood apart, not to cut through it. I am not a perfectionist craft worker – I am a productionist craft worker.

I also like sharp tools that produce a good-quality piece of work, and I emphasize the word 'produce'. I do not have a cabinet full of perfectly sharp chisels that are taken out, polished and replaced. I have working tools that are kept sharp but are in regular use to produce craft.

Defining sharpness

Sharpness is traditionally defined by looking for the 'candle'. Hold a tool in good light, tipping it to and fro as you inspect the edge. A magnifying glass or jeweller's lens can help those of us who are not as sharp sighted as we once were! You are looking for a fine white line along the cutting edge of the tool. This is the 'candle'. The wider the line, the blunter the tool. If there is no candle, the tool is sharp.

Put to good use

I was involved, along with Justin Owen, in producing 60,000 cleft chestnut shakes for the Weald and Downland Museum's Gateway Buildings in Sussex, UK. Three draw knives were in daily use, often working for eight hours a day. These tools needed regular care to keep them in prime condition for the duration of shake making.

Each draw knife may have done more hours of work in a week than many that sit polished in a cupboard do in a lifetime. It was beautiful to see a draw knife that was new at the beginning of the process evolve into looking like an old tool. Months of use saw tannins from the sweet chestnut reacting with the steel and the handles darkened with sweat from the user. This is a tool that was made to be used and is already making its mark in history.

ABOVE: One of the chestnut shake roofs on the Gateway Buildings at the Weald and Downland Museum.

OPPOSITE PAGE: The freshly ground edge of a framing chisel sharpened on an electric water-cooled grindstone.

Grinding

Often done using a grinding machine, grinding is the process of removing metal by an abrasive wheel. It removes metal faster than other techniques and is useful when restoring old tools and when other methods are no longer producing a sharp edge. I use only water-cooled grinding as dry grinding can cause the metal to heat up through friction and risk damaging the temper of the metal.

Using the sandstone water wheel.

The sandstone water wheel at Prickly Nut Wood.

My water wheel

I have an old sandstone water wheel. The trough is cast iron and is marked 'Falkirk Iron Company Ltd 1944' and also shows the War Department 'broad arrow' symbol. The trough is cracked, which is helpful, as it means the water slowly drains out of it and cannot be left full to risk freezing and affecting the part of the wheel that would be submerged. It takes two people to operate the wheel: one to turn the handle and the other to hold the tool at the desired angle. I use it mainly for restoring old tools, in particular old billhooks that are made from quality steel but which have long ago lost their edge.

Smaller wheels

Smaller treadle-operated sandstone wheels can occasionally be found and are operated by one person. Sandstone wheels have been used for thousands of years for grinding. In my village of Lodsworth, not far from my woods is an old quarry that was a major source of quern stones in Iron Age and Roman times. Quern stones were used originally for grinding corn to make flour but later used for working metals. The stones from this quarry have been found across the south-east and southern midlands of England.

Electric wheels

For more precise grinding, I use an electric water-cooled grinding wheel. This has a collection of different jigs designed to hold different tools and a device to set the chosen angle for grinding. Once set up it is a fast and efficient machine and makes rapid progress, dealing with 30 chisels that I need to sharpen prior to teaching a course.

Framing chisel being sharpened on an electric water-cooled grindstone.

Electric water-cooled grindstone.

Keeping it true

Successful grinding relies on the grinding wheel running true. I use a diamond truing tool that fits onto the machine and brings it quickly back into true. The diamond truing tool cuts small grooves as it evens out the stone. I then hold a coarse silicon carbide stone across the wheel while it is turning to remove the grooves.

Honing

This process removes burrs that develop after grinding. It can be done with a selection of stones or leather strops. Honing can be carried out a number of times on a tool to regain sharpness but there will come a time when re-grinding is necessary.

Finding the right stone

I have a stone that was passed on to me, which I call my 'finishing stone'. It is a natural black Arkansas stone from the USA and produces a fine edge. Such stones are hard to come by these days but there are many good alternatives such as Japanese water stones and diamond sharpening 'stones'.

Using a honing stone

Having a suitable honing stone is the starting point. Using it accurately will take practice – when honing a chisel, for example, keeping the bevel flat on the stone, and the angle constant, is not easy. This is where a honing guide is used. There are a large number of honing guides on the market. A honing guide comprises an adjustable clamp to hold the tool at your chosen angle and a roller to guide the tool evenly over the stone.

Diamond sharpening stones

The beauty of the diamond sharpening systems is that the stones stay flat, require virtually no maintenance and are hard enough to sharpen any material. They are expensive. A set of good-quality diamond stones can leave the woodworker with little resources left to buy future tools!

Budget option

I use a low-cost double-sided diamond stone with a coarse 400 grit on one side and a finer 1,000 grit on the other. I do not doubt its limitations compared to some of the top-range diamond sharpening systems but for my needs it is satisfactory. This sits in a non-slip bench holder and I have been impressed with the results.

Using diamond stones

The stones can be a little coarse and abrasive at first but after a little use they soon bed down into a quick and effective sharpening stone. I use water as a lubricant. This removes debris that builds up and cools the sharpening process. I know of woodworkers who use a 50/50 solution of water and alcohol as this dries quicker and reduces the rusting on tools.

Japanese water stones

Of all the available sharpening stones I use, my favourite is the Japanese water stone.

Grades

These stones come in a variety of grades, from 250 grit (very coarse) to 8,000 grit (extra fine). The 8,000 grit is a polishing stone and, although I have no doubt of its virtues, it is a level of sharpening beyond the needs of the tools I use for green woodworking. Working wood green, the wood has not dried out and is fresh and far easier to shape and work than the dried wood that a cabinetmaker would be using. I use combination stones of coarse 250 grit on one side and medium-fine 1,000 grit on the other for many purposes.

Water and maintenance

Japanese stones need to be first saturated in water and then regularly dunked in water during sharpening. They can also be kept permanently in a water container, as this saves re-soaking them prior to use each time. (But be careful not to let the water freeze in cold conditions as this could crack the stones.)

Japanese water stones are soft and will wear away quickly as they are used – re-dressing them with a harder stone can help keep them flat. For any that lose shape after time, I find they make for a useful stone to keep an edge on billhooks while working in the coppice.

LEFT: Electric honing wheels.

ABOVE: A honing guide accurately controlling the angle of the chisel bevel.

BELOW LEFT: Diamond sharpening stone.

BELOW: Japanese water stones.

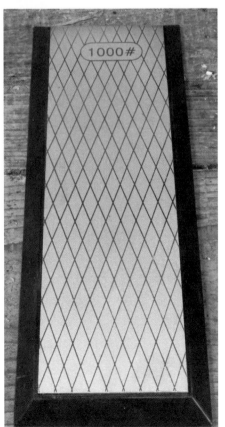

1000#

Strops

Stropping is the process of running your honed tool over a piece of leather that has been first rubbed with a stropping paste or abrasive.

Strops come in many forms and shapes and are used to touch up a tool when the edge has just gone dull. Due to the strops being made of leather, the tool must be drawn back along the strop, lifted and then drawn back again to avoid cutting the leather.

Honing compound

This is a very fine abrasive, which is used when stropping at the final stage of sharpening. The abrasives can be particles of diamond or aluminium oxide, which are bound together sometimes as a paste but more commonly as a bar with wax.

FAR LEFT: A selection of leather strops.

LEFT: Two different wax bars of honing compound, ready to be applied to a leather strop to aid the final phase of sharpening.

A natural strop

If you are in the woods and needing to strop a tool, it is worth looking for the birch polypore fungus *(Piptoporus betulinus)*. The surface has a very similar texture to leather and the polypores were traditionally used for stropping tools, hence the common name, the razor strop fungus. I have used a polypore in the same way as a leather strop and, by drawing a knife over the leathery cap of the fungus, the edge of the blade can be sharpened.

The birch polypore or razor strop fungus can be a useful find.

Drawing a chisel blade across a leather strop, fixed to a wooden base and held firm in a vice.

Grinding a framing chisel on an electric water-cooled grindstone

Sharpening key tools

There are so many different tools that need to be sharpened. In this section the key tools that I use are covered along with the methods I have found that work for me for each tool. This is a starting guide and I am sure you will find techniques that work best for you with the resources you have and the finish you are looking for to carry out your chosen craft.

Using the angle finder to set up a chisel on the grind wheel prior to grinding.

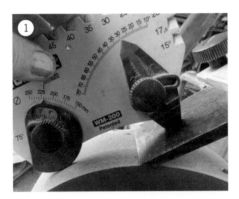

Grinding on the electric water-cooled grindstone.

Honing on the leather strop.

Framing chisels

I sharpen my framing chisels to a 30-degree angle. This seems to be ideal for the type of roundwood timber framing that I do with sweet chestnut. First I use the angle finder I have with my electric water-cooled grindstone. The angle finder is based on the diameter of the grindstone and I adjust this as the stone wears away and the diameter gets smaller.

I then set the angle finder to 30 degrees and place the diameter setting wheel on top of the grindstone and the 30-degree marker on to the chisel, the position of which I can move up and down on the support ①.

Once the setting is right, I then start the grinding wheel and, moving the chisel from side to side along the support, continue to grind until the full bevel of the chisel is silver and freshly ground (you can also grind slicks using the same process) ②. I then like to hone my chisels by hand – this involves drawing them along a leather strop ③.

Framing chisels sharpened and ready for work.

Gouges

My electric water-cooled grindstone has a jig for clamping and holding gouges and I will use this if a gouge is in need of a major sharpen, but as it is fiddly to set up, I prefer to hone them regularly to keep an edge and try and avoid using this grindstone too often.

I use Japanese water stones to hone them. Due to their softness, I have particular stones for particular gouges. Working the gouge to and fro and rotating side to side in the water, the stone will create a sharpening imprint the size of the gouge. The Japanese water stones are soft and each gouge will make its own imprint into the stone. By soaking the stone in water and working each gouge in its particular imprint, a fine edge can be achieved. Larger stones will have room for two or three different-sized imprints, but it is important to use the particular gouge to its size of imprint (1). Cone-shaped water stones enable the inside of the gouge to be lightly honed. I finish the gouges with a rounded leather strop (2).

LEFT: Working a no. 3 sweep gouge in the Japanese water stone imprint.

ABOVE: Using a round leather strop to finish a gouge.

Draw knives

I sharpen my draw knives by grinding them on the electric water-cooled grindstone, using a clamping jig that slides along the support to give an even grind along the whole blade (1). The angle finder can be used to assist setting up. Once ground, I then work the blade over a wet diamond sharpening stone, first at 400 grit and then 1,000 grit to finish (2).

BELOW LEFT: Grinding the draw knife on the electric water-cooled grindstone.

BELOW: Honing the draw knife on the wet diamond stone.

Spoke shaves

I sharpen spoke-shave blades by grinding them on the electric water wheel using the chisel clamping jig ① and then I hone them on a flat 1,000 grit Japanese water stone ②.

BELOW LEFT: Sharpening a spoke-shave blade on the electric water-cooled grindstone.

BELOW: Honing the spoke-shave blade on a Japanese water stone.

Axes

I usually sharpen axes by using a double-sided Japanese water stone of 250 grit and 1,000 grit. I sharpen using a circular motion, first with the coarser 250 grit, and finish with the 1,000 grit ①. If it is a small axe, I will use the axe jig on the electric water-cooled gridstone ② and grind it prior to finishing with the water stone.

BELOW LEFT: Sharpening the axe with the Japanese water stone.

BELOW: Sharpening a side axe on the electric water-cooled grindstone.

Billhooks

I sharpen billhooks using a double-sided Japanese water stone of 250 grit and 1,000 grit. I sharpen first the shoulder of the blade with the 250 grit side, then the edge of the billhook and then repeat with the 1,000 grit to finish. Turn the billhook upside down to sharpen the other side, so that you are never sharpening towards the blade.

OPPOSITE PAGE: Sharpening a billhook with a Japanese water stone – notice that I am working away from the edge of the blade.

Hook knives

For sharpening hook knives, I have a small curved Japanese water stone that works well. If you have a very curved knife, wrapping different grades of silicon carbide paper around a thin dowel can be very effective. Start with a 250 grit if the knife needs a good sharpen and work up to 1,000 or 1,500 grit. Finish by stropping with a round leather strop; again, leather stuck to a dowel and rubbed with honing compound is ideal. With both the papers and the strop, remember to push away from the blade.

RIGHT: Hook knife with silicon carbide paper on a dowel and curved leather strop.

Froes

I rarely sharpen my froes unless they seem very blunt when cleaving a piece of wood. If I do need to sharpen them, I work them on my old sandstone water wheel. The exception to this is my lath froe, which needs to be sharper as it needs to start cleaving through thin strips of wood. If it is very blunt, I will place it on the electric water-cooled grindstone and grind the edge and then hone the edge of the lath froe with a 250 grit Japanese water stone. This will make it sharp enough and it should then just need regular touch-ups from the Japanese water stone.

RIGHT: Sharpening the lath froe on the electric water-cooled grindstone.

Chainsaws

First check the chain teeth are of even size and that the chain has not been sharpened beyond the 'witness lines' on the top of each tooth. These are an angled line on the top of each tooth, which mark the point that you must not sharpen beyond. If it is down to or beyond the witness lines, replace the chain. Next, using a flat file, file off any burrs on the chainsaw bar and check that the rails that run around the bar that the chain sits on are level. If they are not, your saw will not cut straight. Level the rails if necessary with a flat file.

To sharpen a chain, put the bar and chain back on the saw, tension the chain to normal use and clamp the chainsaw bar in a vice. I use soft jaws on my vice for this. Next, using a coloured pen, colour in the top of one of the teeth; this is so you are clear where you started sharpening and to ensure you don't sharpen some teeth more than others. Each tooth should be filed evenly. Check you have the right-sized diameter round file for the chain on your saw. It is best to use a file guide with the file as this has angles marked on it.

File each tooth at 30 degrees. I recommend a maximum of two strokes on each tooth – you don't want to file away that chain too quickly! Once one side is completed, turn the saw around in the vice and repeat the process on the other side.

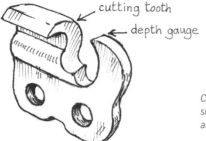

Chainsaw chain link showing cutting edge and depth gauge.

BELOW: Sharpening the chainsaw teeth using a round file and file guide. Note the tooth coloured orange to the left of the tooth being sharpened – this is the starting point.

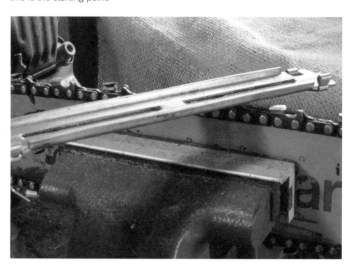

Filing down the depth gauge

Each time you sharpen the saw teeth, the depth gauge setting will gradually become too high. Every third time you sharpen the chain, you should file down the depth gauge. This is done with a depth-gauge tool and a flat file. You place the depth gauge tool over the chain and use the flat file to file off the tip of the depth-gauge that protrudes through the depth gauge tool.

Using the depth-gauge tool and flat file to file down the depth gauge.

PEELERS AND KNEE VICES

*This is a selection of devices that are used for peeling
long poles with large diameters. The roundwood peeler
was developed for peeling large roundwood framing
poles. The peeling jig takes smaller diameter long poles
with the craftworker peeling them from a standing
position with the pole held in a horizontal position.
The two knee vices work with long poles held vertically,
allowing the craftworker to sweep down with a draw
knife while clamping the pole in position with their knee.*

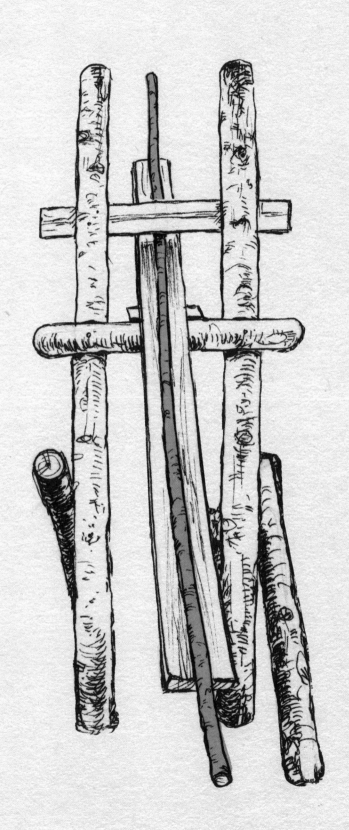

Draw knifing a timber-framing pole supported on a roundwood peeler.

ROUNDWOOD PEELER

The roundwood peeler is a simple device I have been using in the woods for a number of years – it is particularly useful when peeling large poles. Most workshop devices are designed for clamping and holding small pieces of wood for detailed work whereas the roundwood peeler is ideal for peeling timber framing poles.

Materials you will need

Any strong roundwood can be used but sweet chestnut or ash would be preferable.

2 lengths of roundwood for the sides of the 'A' frame:
55in (1400mm) long x 4in (100mm) diameter
1 length of roundwood for the cross beam:
51in (1300mm) long x 4in (100mm) diameter
1 length of roundwood for the support leg:
43in (1100mm) long x 4in (100mm) diameter
1 length of threaded bar:
20in (500mm) long x ½in (12mm) diameter
4 nuts: to fit threaded bar
Hemp rope: 60in (1500mm) long x ½in (12mm) diameter
Timber lock fixings or coach screws: 6 x 6in (150mm)

Recommended tools

Panel saw, hack saw, drill, drill auger bit ⅝in (15mm), drill pilot bit ¼in (6mm), impact driver, metal file.

Making the 'A' frame

Choose a level surface and lay one leg over the top of the other so that the angle where they cross is approximately 60 degrees. Chock up the base of the top leg with a 4in (100mm) block so the legs are levelled ①. Pilot drill two holes where the pole cross and using the impact driver fix with 2 x 6in (150mm) timber locks.

Lay the cross beam across the base of the legs and then pilot drill and fix with 2 x 6in (150mm) timber locks into each leg. Your frame should now resemble ②.

LEFT: Laying out the 'A' frame with one leg chocked, so they are level for fixing.

RIGHT: The 'A' frame completed.

Hold the support leg between the two 'A' frame legs under where they cross one another (an extra person helps here) and drill through all three pieces of timber with the 5/8in (15mm) auger bit. Take time to eye up all three pieces before drilling to ensure the auger bit goes close to the centre of all three pieces of wood ③.

Pass the threaded bar through the hole connecting all three pieces. Put two nuts on each end and tighten each nut to the one in front ④. Cut the threaded bar with the hacksaw to length and file sharp edges with a flat file.

Next, drill a 5/8in (15mm) hole with the auger bit at the midpoint of the crossbeam and through the support leg 4in (100mm) up from the base of the leg. Thread through the rope and tie a knot at each end ⑤. The length of the rope will dictate the angle of the peeler. The roundwood peeler is now ready to use ⑥.

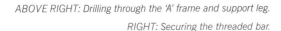
ABOVE RIGHT: Drilling through the 'A' frame and support leg.

RIGHT: Securing the threaded bar.

LEFT: Securing the rope.

RIGHT: The completed roundwood peeler.

PEELING JIG

This peeling jig is one I have returned to many a time when
I have a large number of small diameter poles to peel. It can
be constructed quickly and can be easily adapted to the length
of product that you are peeling.

Materials you will need

2 posts: 72in (1828mm) long x 6in (150mm) diameter
2 poles for braces: 96in (2438mm) long x 3in (75mm) diameter
The length of the thinner poles will create the size of peeling jig you require. These measurements are for peeling 120in (3048mm) long poles. If you reduce the length of the thinner poles the jig will work for peeling shorter lengths.
Timber locks: 6in (150mm)

Recommended tools

Post rammer or sledge hammer, axe, gouge, maul, saw, impact driver, drill, ¼in (6mm) auger bit, draw knife.

Peeling jig history

The vast majority of chestnut coppice in the UK is in Kent, Sussex and Surrey, partly due to the traditional growing of hops in this region. Hop gardens were abundant in the south-east and they needed durable vertical poles for the hops to grow up. Chestnut was the perfect timber and continued to be used in hop gardens until concrete posts and steel wires replaced the chestnut poles.

Using a peeling jig to peel hop poles in the chestnut coppice near Goudhurst in Kent, 1947.

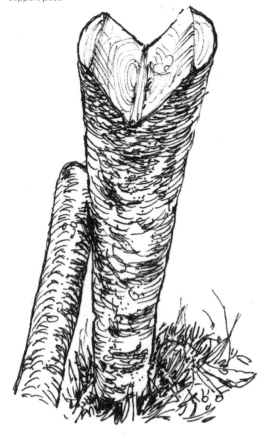

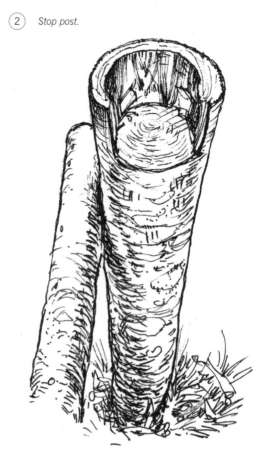

Support posts

Take the two posts and point the ends using an axe. Drive the posts into the ground until they are stable with either a post rammer or sledge hammer. I prefer to use a post rammer as there is less chance of splitting the post. The distance between the posts will determine the length of material to be worked. I like to set the distance at least 12in (300mm) shorter than the length of material that I am peeling.

Now choose your working height. I like to work at a height of 46in (1170mm) from the ground when peeling with a draw knife. You may prefer a higher or lower height depending upon how tall you are. Saw the posts level at your chosen working height.

Bracing posts

You now need to attach the thinner poles to brace the posts. These braces are fixed diagonally from the top of one post to the base of the other on opposite sides. Make sure they are fixed at least 5in (125mm) below the working height that you have sawn of the posts at. Pre-drill each brace with the ¼in (6mm) auger bit and secure with the impact driver and timber locks.

Saw a 'V' shape in the top of the support post ①. This must be deep enough for the diameter of the material you are peeling to sit in.

Shaping the stop post

Using a maul and gouge, chisel out the stop post so that the thicker end of the material will sit comfortably against the back of the 'stop' you have carved out ②. Place your material in the jig and draw knife back towards the stop post ③. You now have a completed peeling jig ④.

Chiselling out the stop post.

The completed peeling jig.

The peeling jig in use.

SUSSEX KNEE VICE

This powerful clamping vice is useful for holding lengths that are too long for a shaving horse. I use a knee vice for peeling yurt poles and rustic furniture poles, anything from about 1in (25mm) to 3in (75mm) diameter will work well in this knee vice. My design is an adaption from early pictures of knee vices I have come across.

Materials you will need

1 length of slab wood for the bed: 89in (2260mm) long x 9½in (241mm) wide x 3½in (89mm) deep. I used slab wood as I had some lengths of chestnut available. You could also cleave out a large log of about 10in (254mm) diameter and work one half with the axe to create the bed.

1 length of sawn timber for the lever plank: 4in (100mm) long x 3in (75mm) wide x 75in (1905mm) deep. This again could be shaped out of a cleft piece of timber. I chose a piece of Douglas fir for this project, mainly because its colour would contrast with the chestnut to help clarify the different parts in the pictures.

Seasoned oak for the pegs:
36in (914mm) long x 1½in (38mm) wide x 1½in (38mm) deep

2 poles for the legs: 50in (127mm) long x 2½in (64mm) diameter

1 bucket

Cord: 40in (1016mm) long x ¼in (6mm) diameter

Sand: small amount to add to the bucket

Recommended tools

Chainsaw, draw knife, shaving horse, 1in (25mm) rounding plane, spoke shave, 1in (25mm) and ½in (12mm) auger bits, drill, chisel, maul, axe, plane, protractor, sliding bevel.

Showing the process of loading the Sussex knee vice with a pole to be worked through to clamping and draw knifing the pole.

Sussex knee vice history

Sussex has a strong coppicing tradition, which still survives to this day. This craftsman is peeling poles for hoops with a draw knife. Hoops made from hazel or chestnut were in strong demand for securing dry barrels. Dry barrels were used for transportation of non-liquid produce like fruit, cheese and sugar. All components could be used a large number of times and when the dry barrel came to the end of its life it could be used for firewood, and yet we thought plastic was progress!

A Sussex knee vice in operation near Petworth in 1937.

Laying the lever plank on the slab wood bed for marking.

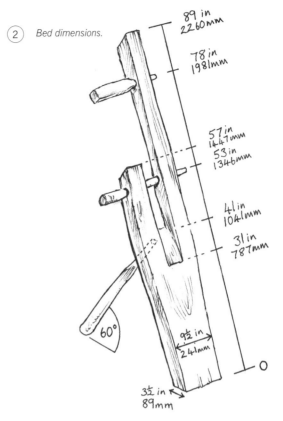

(2) *Bed dimensions.*

89 in
2260mm

78 in
1981mm

57 in
1447mm

53 in
1346mm

41 in
1041mm

31 in
787mm

60°

9½ in
241mm

0

3½ in
89mm

Adapting to fit

Traditional Sussex knee vices seem to pivot on a metal insert that is notched into the lever plank. I have decided to move away from using the metal and to incorporate a pivot peg as I like the action and stability gained from having a peg inserted right through the lever plank. The strength of grip is excellent and if, like me, you often like to work in a standing position rather than a sitting position, this knee vice may become a personal favourite.

The standing position with one knee pressing the lever board is surprisingly comfortable, although if you were using it for days at a time, a knee pad or some sheep's wool wrapped around the lever board at the point of contact with the knee might be a good addition. Despite the bulk of the knee vice, it dismantles easily and can be moved from place to place with relative ease.

Bed

My chosen piece of slab wood for the bed was far from straight but by laying the lever plank on top of the bed, I could mark the sides of the lever plank and know where the slot would fall (1). See drawing (2) for the bed dimensions. Next, use the chainsaw to roughly cut out the shape of the bed (3). Using a draw knife and a plane, clean up the bed.

The bed roughly chainsawed out.

PLEASE ENSURE YOU ARE TRAINED IN USING A CHAINSAW AND ARE WEARING THE RELEVANT CHAINSAW SAFETY KIT (PPE) BEFORE CARRYING OUT THIS TASK.

Making the tenon on the end of one of the legs using the rounding plane.

Legs

I made the legs from rounds rather than cleft wood as they will be taken in and out of the bed as it is moved from one place to another and I imagine they will need replacing after a few years, so I decided to go for a quick and simple option. Using a draw knife, taper the end of the legs until the end is thin enough to fit into the 1in (25mm) rounding plane. Create a 2in- (50mm)-long tenon on the end of each leg ④.

Lay the bed upside down and, using the protractor and sliding bevel, set the angle for the legs at 60 degrees. Drill the mortices into the bed 41in (1041mm) from the bottom of the bed. The legs should splay out from the bed, so the drilling angle is a compound angle. Insert the legs into the bed and tap them home with the maul ⑤. The bed should now stand up ⑥. The angle of the bed and the legs may vary slightly depending on your height and preferred upright angle of working.

Pivot peg

Drill through the bed across the slot with the 1in (25mm) auger bit to create the hole for the pivot peg ⑦. Using a draw knife and shaving horse, whittle down an oak blank and, using the 1in (25mm) rounding plane, create the pivot peg. Leave one end fat and then, using the spoke shave, shave the peg down further as it needs to be able to be inserted and removed with relative ease.

While making the pivot peg, this is a good time to also prepare the stop peg. This peg needs partially rounding to 1in (25mm), so that it can be inserted through the tall section of the bed, but the rest of it left as a square blank ⑧.

The legs inserted into the bed.

The bed standing.

Drilling the hole for the pivot peg with the 1in (25mm) auger bit.

The pivot peg (left) and stop peg (right).

3in (75mm)

75 in 1905mm

48 in 1219mm

37½ in 952mm

4 in 100 mm

2 in 50mm

0

Lever plank

Halfway along the plank, make a 1in (25mm) deep angled cut and then rip saw 1in (25mm) from one end of the plank, so that half of the plank measures 4in (100mm) x 3in (75mm) and the other half measures 4in (100mm) x 2in (50mm) 9 10.

Offer the lever plank into the slot and mark where to drill for the pivot peg to pass through the lever plank. This should be 48in (1219mm) from the thinner end of the lever plank. Drill the lever plank and insert the pivot peg through the bed and lever plank. The lever plank should swing freely but will not sit flat enough to the bed at this stage for the top of the lever plank to reach the position of the stop peg 11.

Shaping the lever plank.

The lever plank fixed to the bed with the pivot peg.

Extending the slot

Using a saw, maul and chisel, extend the slot so that the lever plank sits flatter to the bed and the top of the lever plank lines up so that the position of the stop peg can be determined (12). Mark this position and, using the 1in (25mm) auger, drill the hole for the stop peg (13). Insert the stop peg and test the knee vice for its grip by inserting a workpiece between the lever plank and the stop peg (14).

Extending the slot with a framing chisel.

The extended slot.

The stop peg in position.

Adding counterbalance

Drill a ½in (12mm) hole in the top of the lever plank and thread through the cord and secure to the bucket handle. Add sand to the bucket until the lever plank gently swings into an open position. This will mean that whenever you remove your knee from the lever plank the vice will open. When you press your knee against the lever plank, the vice closes, locking the pole in position to peel (15). This gives great control and speed for turning your workpiece. You should now be ready to use the knee vice (16).

The knee vice closed with workpiece clamped.

The lever plank in horizontal position with the vice held open by the bucket counterbalance.

Peelers and knee vices   **81**

Peeling a yurt pole using a draw knife
on the ladder knee vice.

LADDER KNEE VICE

This ladder knee vice is quick and easy to construct and, although it is not portable, if set up in the right place it is a powerful gripping vice, ideal for peeling longer poles. It makes a good choice for peeling yurt poles, rustic furniture poles, split palisade and gate hurdles.

Materials you will need

2 poles: 126in (3200mm) long x 5in (125mm) diameter
1 pole to cleave for the brake: 36in (914mm) long x 4in (100mm) diameter
2 poles for the braces: 56in (1422mm) long x 4in (100mm) diameter
1 length of sawn timber for the lever plank: 94in (2387mm) long x 8in (200mm) wide x 1½in (38mm) deep
1 piece of sawn timber for the pivot: 14in (356mm) long x 3in (75mm) wide x 2in (50mm) deep
Timber locks or coach screws: 4in (100mm) and 6in (150mm)

Recommended tools

Spade, tamper, froe, maul, cleaving brake, spirit level, saw, chisel, drill, impact driver, ¼in (6mm) auger bit, panel saw.

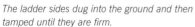

The ladder sides dug into the ground and then tamped until they are firm.

Cleaving the pole to make the rungs of the vice.

Poles and rungs

Dig two holes 24in (610mm) deep and 21in (533mm) apart and insert the two tall poles for the ladder sides. Using the tamper, firm up the ground around each of the poles (1). With the froe and cleaving brake, cleave the 36in (914mm) pole in two to make the horizontal rungs of the vice (2).

Marking the ladder rungs

Following drawing (3), use a spirit level to mark the positions of where the rungs will be fitted to the ladder sides (4). Offer the rungs to the marked positions and draw onto the ladder sides where they cross.

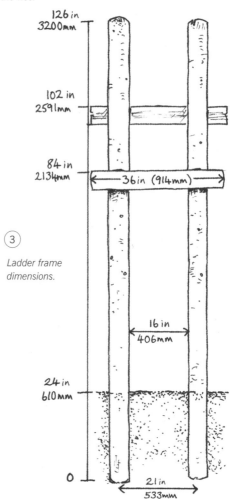

(3)

Ladder frame dimensions.

126 in
3200mm

102 in
2591mm

84 in
2134mm — 36in (914mm)

16 in
406mm

24 in
610mm

21 in
533mm

0

Using a spirit level to mark the positions for the horizontal rungs.

Chiselling out the flats in the ladder sides to receive the cleaved horizontal rungs.

Fixing the rungs

Using first the panel saw and then the maul and chisel, create flats in the ladder sides so that the rungs will have maximum contact ⑤. Pre-drill with the ¼in (6mm) auger and fix the rungs with timber locks or coach screws ⑥.

Completed ladder frame.

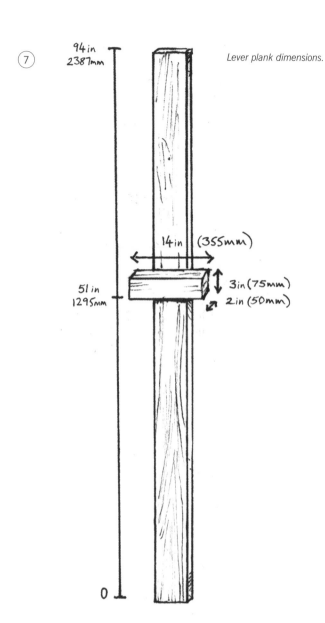

(7) 94in
2387mm

Lever plank dimensions.

14in (355mm)

51in
1295mm

3in (75mm)
2in (50mm)

0

(8)

Fixing the pivot to the lever plank.

(9)

The lever plank

Before offering up the lever plank to the ladder frame, check that the length of the plank and the position of the pivot is correct for your body size. The measurements in (7) are based on my height of 71in (1803mm) and may need adjustment if you are taller or shorter. Mark the position for the pivot on the lever plank and pre-drill and fix the pivot (8). You can now offer the lever plank to the ladder frame (9)(10).

The lever plank and frame brought together.

Showing the pivot position from the rear of the ladder.

Braces attached to the ladder.

Bracing poles

Add the bracing poles to help stabilize the ladder knee vice once work begins (11). I find the shaving position and angle on this vice to be very ergonomic (12). The ladder knee vice is now ready to use (13).

Shaving a pole clamped in the vice.

The completed ladder knee vice.

SHAVING HORSES

Whether experienced or totally new to woodland crafts, the one device that gets more regular use than any other is the shaving horse. This is an essential part of any woodland workshop and the design you choose will be both dependent on the crafts you are making and the ergonomics of the horse that works best for you and your build. I have offered guidance for the making of four different shaving horses, each of which is a thoroughbred in its own right.

EASY RIDER
SHAVING HORSE

The Easy Rider shaving horse was designed by Sean Hellman
to create a more ergonomic shaving horse than many of the
traditional designs. It has an adjustable seat so that the same
horse can be used by adults and children and with the ability
to work closer or further away from your piece of work.

Draw knifing in comfort on the ergonomic Easy Rider shave horse.

Materials you will need

1 log for bed: minimum 70in (1780mm) long
x 8in (200mm) diameter
2 logs for platform block and seat frame: 24in (600mm) long
x 8in (200mm) diameter
2 logs for legs: 42in (1070mm) long x 2½in (64mm) diameter
1 seasoned plank for seat and foot plate: 40in (1016mm) long
x 12½in wide (320mm) x 1½in (38mm) deep
3 pieces of seasoned oak for pegs: 18in (450mm) long
x 1½in (38mm) wide x 1½in (38mm) deep
1 piece of forked timber for combined lever post and top jaw:
at least 36in (915mm) long and 5in (125mm) diameter
Stainless steel ring shank nails: a few 1½in (38mm) size

Recommended tools

Panel saw, ripsaw, draw knife, drill, 1in (25mm), ⅝in (15mm) and
½in (12mm) auger bits, spoke shave, 1in (25mm) and ⅝in (15mm)
rounding plane, 2 large clamps, chisel, chalk line, axe and splitting
wedges, plane, 2 sliding bevels, reamer, chain morticer (helpful
but not essential).

All of these timber sizes can
be transferred to sawn wood
dimensions and made from
oak or Douglas fir. If making a
sawn wood version, the lever
post and top jaw will need to be
jointed together.

Visit from the designer

I first met Sean over 30 years ago, whittling wood
at the start of his green woodworking career. Based
in south Devon, UK, where he makes a wide range
of craft produce and tools, he is now established
as a teacher and innovator and has inspired many
students with both his knowledge of craft and
creativity of products.

Sean's particular passion is for the shaving horse
and the Easy Rider is testament to his research and
practice and all green woodworkers will benefit from
this new arrival to the stable. He came to visit me at
Prickly Nut Wood and made this shave horse from
seasoned and windblown sweet chestnut coppice.
With a shaving horse of this design, shrinkage and
movement of wood is not recommended, hence the
choice of seasoned timber rather than green.

Sean was keen to work with what was available and
we spent a few hours looking for appropriate shapes
amongst the windblown chestnut, in particular
looking for lever posts with a fork that included
the top jaw in the same piece of wood. Windblown
chestnut can be full of interestingly shaped branches.
These can yield many potential lever posts. The
nature of sweet chestnut with its small amount of
sapwood and high durability mean that beneath
the sapwood layer the wood will be sound.

Sean Hellman visiting Prickly Nut Wood.

Cleaving and marking the bed

Using our collection of wood (see box opposite), Sean cleaved out the chestnut pole to make the bed ① . There was a slight twist in the cleave but we chose the better half and Sean began to axe down the cleaved face to get a flat surface ② . Next we used a chalk line to mark out two parallel lines ③ and with the axe worked to the lines to create approximate parallel square sides on the bed in relation to the cleaved face ④ ⑤ ⑥ .

The bed, cleaved with axe and wedges.

Sean working the cleaved face of the bed with an axe to create a flat face.

The bed is marked with parallel chalk lines 5in (125mm) apart.

Sean working with the axe to the chalk lines.

The bed with parallel sides.

⑥   Dimensions of the lever post with incorporated top jaw.

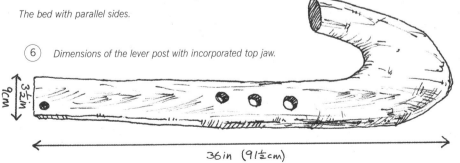

12in (30cm)

3½in
9cm

36in (91½cm)

Windblown chestnut provides ideal shapes for lever posts.

⑦

Squaring off the sides of the lever post.

⑧ *Bed dimensions.*

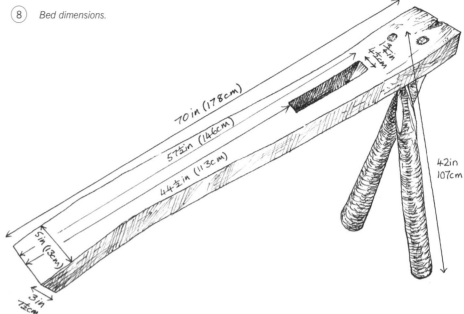

70in (178cm)

57½in (146cm)

44½in (113cm)

1¾in 4.5cm

5in (13cm)

3in 7½cm

42in 107cm

Squaring off and marking the mortice slot

Square off the incorporated lever post and top jaw with the axe until the post is 1¾in (45mm) wide ⑦. This measurement can then be used to mark out the mortice slot on the bed. See drawing ⑧ for its exact position.

Cutting the mortice slot

The mortice can be cut in a number of ways. It can be done totally with chisels, or by drill and chisel – the drill making a number of holes and the chisel finishing off removing the waste – or by chain morticer. For this project we opted for the chain morticer for ease and accuracy. The mortice we cut measured 13in (330mm) long by 1¾in (45mm) ⑨. With the bed morticed, check the lever post is a good fit by inserting it into the mortice. Make any small adjustments at this stage.

⑨

Using the chain morticer to cut the mortice in the bed.

Using the rounding plane to make the leg tenons.

Setting up the sliding bevels to drill out the compound angle for the legs.

The bed with the holes drilled for the legs and the mortice slot for the lever post cut.

Making the legs

For this we used two chestnut rounds. Using a rounding plane, create a 1in (25mm) diameter tenon on the end of each leg (10). Being made from small diameter roundwood, the legs will radially split and may need replacing after a number of years. For longer-lasting legs that will not split, a log should be cleft into quarters and each quarter whittled down to make the legs.

Making the leg holes

The holes for the legs need to be carefully drilled out to avoid drilling too close to the edge of the wood. The finished angle for the bed is 30 degrees, so we clamped the bed at this angle prior to drilling for the legs. The legs are drilled at a compound angle 20 degrees to the side and 20 degrees backwards, measured with the bed clamped at its finished angle.

Use two sliding bevels to set the leg angles (these can be clamped to the bed) – it is helpful to have another person to 'eye in' the auger bit to the sliding bevel angles (11).

Getting the right fit

At this stage consider how tight you want the legs to fit. Is this to be a shave horse permanently set up? Or is it a shave horse you are going to travel around with? If it is the latter you will need to remove and put back the legs on regular occasions and therefore spoke shaving a little more off the leg tenons should be carried out prior to fitting the legs (12). Once you have made your choice, insert the legs into the bed (13).

The bed with legs inserted at its finished angle of 30 degrees.

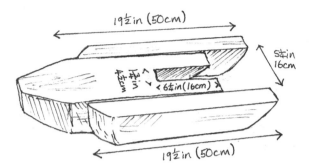

(14) *Platform block dimensions.*

19½in (50cm)

5¼in 16cm

6¼in (16cm)

19½in (50cm)

Rip sawing the slot.   *Finishing the slot with a chisel.*

Starting the platform block

Cleave out an 8in (200mm) diameter chestnut log and square off the sides using the axe to create a block the same width as the bed – in this case, 5in (125mm) (14). Using a ripsaw, cut a 30-degree angle so that the platform block should sit on the bed and the top of the platform should be level. Using the ripsaw and chisel, cut out the slot in the platform to the same width as the mortice in the bed – in this case, 1¾in (45mm) (15) (16). Offer the platform block up to the bed to check the slot and mortice line up (17).

Making a tenon and mortice

Cleave out a piece of wood and square it up with an axe to approximately 3in (75mm) square and then create a 2 x 2in (50 x 50mm) tenon on one end of the piece of wood. This tenon should also be about 2in (50mm) deep (18). Turn over the platform block and draw around the tenon on the underside of the platform block to mark out where to cut the mortice. The centre of the mortice is approximately 5in (125mm) from the back edge of the slot.

Chisel out the mortice and fit the mortice and tenon together (19). This can be drilled and pegged with a 5/8in (16mm) auger and then a 5/8in (15mm) peg inserted. The peg can be cut off flush to the edges of the platform block as there are sides to fit that will cover the ends of the peg.

Saw the block of wood off at 30 degrees, marking and lining up the saw with the 30-degree angle cut on the end of the platform block (20).

Making the sides and peg

Cleave out two pieces of wood for the sides, 20in (510mm) long x 3½in (89mm) wide x 1½in (38mm) deep and clean up using a draw knife or plane to create a pair of even-sized blocks of wood. Make a 1in (25mm) peg by whittling down the oak with a draw knife and using the 1in (25mm) rounding plane to create the peg.

Offering up the platform block to the bed.

Drawing around the tenon to mark out for the mortice.

Chiselling out the mortice.

Sawing the block at 30 degrees.

Clamping the sides and platform block to the bed and drilling out and inserting the peg.

Marking parallel lines across the sides and the platform block to guide the drilling process.

Reaming out the edges of the holes.

Cutting a slot in the peg with a chisel.

Peg holes

Offer the platform block and the sides to the bed, clamping the sides in place. Drill a level 1in (25mm) hole (an extra person helps for eyeing the auger bit) through the sides and the bed and insert the peg you have made through it ㉑. Again, make sure the peg isn't too tight as you will need to get it out again.

Draw two parallel lines across the sides and the platform block 3 ½in (89mm) apart ㉒ and drill out two 1in (25mm) holes through the sides and platform block following the parallel lines as a guide. Ream the edges of the holes ㉓ and insert another 1in (25mm) oak peg into each of the holes. Cut the pegs off flush to the sides and, using a chisel, cut a thin slot across the peg ㉔. Insert an oak wedge and hammer it in ㉕. Finish by cutting the excess of the wedge off flush.

Wedging the peg.

With holes drilled through the bed mortice, the lever post is offered up for drilling.

Drilling out the lever post.

Pivot peg inserted through platform block, bed and lever post.

Inserting the lever post

Drill two parallel 1in (25mm) holes through the mortice on the bed – in this case, 4½in (114mm) apart. These are to give different options for the position of the lever post. Insert the lever post into the mortice and find a position where it pivots easily (26) and drill through the lever post using one of the holes you have already drilled through the mortice on the bed (27).

A number of further holes can be drilled into the lever post to give different options for height of the top jaw above the platform block depending upon the size of material you are clamping. Now insert the pivot peg through the sides of the platform block, the bed and the lever post (28).

Seat rails

Cleave out two more blocks of wood for the seat rails, 20in (510mm) long x 1½in (38mm) thick x 3½in (90mm)

wide in the same way you made the sides for the platform block (29). Clamp them together and drill a hole through both rails 4½in (114mm) from one end. Clamp the seat rails to the bed and tap in a 1in (25mm) oak peg through the holes but under the bed (30).

Mark the angle of the bed onto the seat rails by drawing a line on the inside of the rails following the angle of the bed. Clamp the seat rails together again and tap the oak peg through the existing holes. Mark the position for drilling the hole through both rails for the second peg (31). Note that the position of this second peg is dictated by the angle you have drawn and that the two pegs are offset (32).

This is to allow the seat to grip the bed when it is slid into your chosen position. Next drill out the second 1in (25mm) hole and fix the pegs with the rails in position on the bed. Drill and fix 1½in (38mm) stainless steel ring shank nails through the rails and into the peg to maintain their position. Cut the pegs off flush to the seat rails.

(29)   *Dimensions from the underside of the seat, including seat rails.*

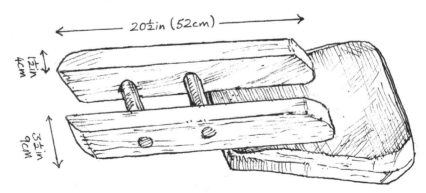

20½in (52cm)

1½in 4cm

3½in 9cm

Marking the bed angle onto the inside of the seat rails.

Marking the position for drilling the second hole.

The pegs fitted through the seat rails – note the offset position.

Connecting the rail to the seat plank

Shape the seat plank ③③ with a saw, chisel and plane and lay the pegged rails on the seat plank, ensuring both pegs are visible and that the peg closest to the seat is not obscured by the front of the seat plank ③④.

Mark the position of the seat rails on the underside of the seat plank and then clamp the seat rails and seat plank together in their finished position and fix the rails to the seat ③⑤. This can be done either with stainless steel fixings (remember to pre-drill) or by pegging with seasoned oak pegs at an offset angle.

Using oak pegs

For this project, oak pegs were used. Angle drill with a ½in (12mm) auger bit and fix with ½in (12mm) oak pegs. The angle of the drill should be offset for each peg, so that the pegs are skewed – a little wood glue could help to fix them in place. Hammer the pegs home and cut off flush to the seat top ③⑥.

Moving the seat

The seat can now be slid up the bed and should lock in any position you choose, so that you have flexibility to sit at any height ③⑦.

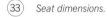
③③ Seat dimensions.

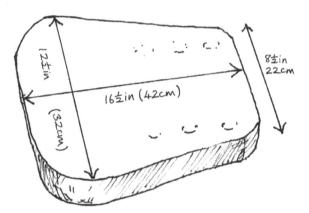

Laying the seat rails over the seat plank.

Marking the rail positions on the underside of the seat.

Seat plank and seat rails being attached with skew oak pegs.

The finished seat in position on the bed.

Footplate

Lay the lever post centrally on top of the footplate plank and mark the edges of the lever post to obtain the correct size for the mortice slot (38)(39). Using the ripsaw cut out the mortice slot and check with the lever post that it is a good fit (40). The back edge of the mortice slot should be angled to coincide with the position of the lever post. This is best worked out by offering the footplate to the lever post while the lever post is attached to the bed and the platform block.

Cleave out a block of wood 12in (300mm) long x 2in (50mm) wide x 2in (50mm) deep. Ripsaw the block so that it creates a half dovetail profile and offer this up to the lever post and footplate plank. Cut a slot into the footplate at the angle of the half dovetail and chisel out the slot. The half dovetail block will now hold the footplate in place (41).

Finally drill a ½in (12mm) hole through the lever post directly under the footplate and insert a ½in (12mm) oak peg to hold the footplate in place (42). Assemble all the parts and your Easy Rider shaving horse will be ready for work (43).

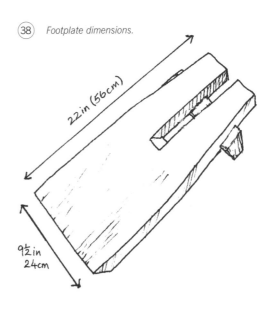

(38)   *Footplate dimensions.*

22in (56cm)

9½in
24cm

Marking the position of the mortice slot on the footplate.

Checking the fit of the lever post into the footplate.

The half-dovetailed block holding the footplate to the lever post.

FAR LEFT: The peg inserted into the lever post that secures the footplate in place.

LEFT: The Easy Rider shaving horse.

DUMBHEAD SHAVING HORSE

This European design has a strong grip due to the lever post being pivoted near the top of the shaving horse, whereas the traditional English shaving horse pivots closer to the centre. Both are vices that work for making a variety of different products but over time I have come to favour the Dumbhead due to its extra grip strength.

Shaping a peg blank on a Dumbhead shaving horse.

Materials you will need

I used oak for this project as I have a store of milled planks seasoning. Other timbers such as Douglas fir would also be fine.

1 seasoned plank for the bed: 55in (1397mm) long x 1in (330mm) wide x 2in (50mm) deep

1 seasoned plank for the footplate: 20in (508mm) long x 9½in (241mm) wide x 2in (50mm) deep

1 seasoned plank for the platform: 28in (711mm) long x 8½in (216mm) wide x 2in (50mm) deep

1 seasoned plank for the platform supports: 16in (400mm) long x 8in (200mm) wide x 2in (50mm) deep

Seasoned oak for pegs and wedges: 24in (600mm) long x 1in (25mm) wide x 1in (25mm) deep

1 log for the legs (preferably chestnut or ash): 24in (600mm) long x 8in (200mm) diameter

Right-angled piece of wood for the lever post: 32½in (825mm) long x 3½in (89mm) wide x 12in (300mm) length of the opposing angle

Stainless steel ring shank nails: 4 x 1¾in (45mm)

Stainless steel timber locks: 8 x 4in (100mm)

Recommended tools

Axe, splitting wedges, draw knife, shaving horse or vice, 1in (25mm), ¾in (19mm) and ⅝in (15mm) rounding planes, plane, callipers, chisel, maul, drill, 1in (25mm), ¾in (19mm), ⅝in (15mm) and ¼in (6mm) auger bits, impact driver, chainsaw or jigsaw, protractor, sliding bevel, Japanese saw, spoke shave, spirit level, deep throat clamp.

Legs

Cleave out the 8in (100mm) diameter log into quarters using splitting wedges (1)(2). I start my splits off with an old axe head and then follow the cleave with wedges. Choose the best three, if you are making a three-leg shaving horse.

Draw a 1½in (38mm) diameter circle on the end grain of each leg. I use a piece of plumbing pipe for this but any circular object of this diameter will be fine (3)(4).

Axe down each leg blank to form a tapered billet. Work with the draw knife and bring each leg to a taper towards the circle on the end grain (5). Whittle down the tapered end until it fits into the wide end of the 1in (25mm) rounding plane and with the rounding plane create a 2¼in (57mm) length of round tenon on the end of each leg (6).

Three legs are good

All of my shaving horses have three legs because much of their work is carried out in the woods on uneven ground and three legs are more stable, but if your shaving horse is to be used solely in the workshop then a four-leg version may suit you better. If you decide to make a four-leg version, ignore the angles for fitting the front leg and repeat the process and angles I suggest for the back legs.

Cleaving out a round pole using an axe head to start the cleave.

Cleaving the half rounds into quarters to form the leg billets.

Using a piece of pipe to mark a circle as a guide for the leg tenon.

The circle clearly visible on the end grain.

Shaping the leg with a draw knife.

Using the rounding plane to create the leg tenon.

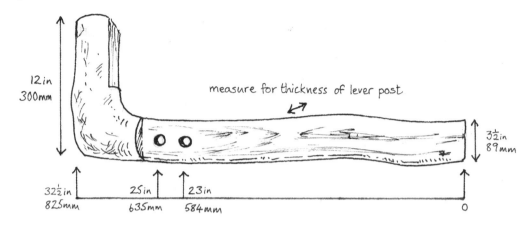

(7) *Lever post dimensions.*

12 in
300mm

measure for thickness of lever post

$3\frac{1}{2}$in
89mm

$32\frac{1}{2}$in
825mm

25in
635mm

23in
584mm

0

Axing down the opposing sides of the lever post.

Lever post

As with the Easy Rider shaving horse (see page 92), this horse will have a combined lever post and top jaw for extra strength (7). For this, I chose a right-angled piece of chestnut. Axe down the opposing sides of the longer part of the lever post and then check with callipers that the width is even on each side (8) (9). Draw knife the sides to get them as even as possible and then use this measurement as the width for cutting the mortice slot into the bed.

Checking the width of the lever post is even with callipers.

Bed

Take the plank for the bed and plane out any obvious high points. I made the bed, platform and supports out of one large plank I had. It had cupped a little at one end and I put that part to one side to use as the platform supports and used the flattest parts for the bed and platform. I then roughly shaped the bed using a chainsaw (a jigsaw would also be fine).

Using the calliper measurement of the thickness of the lever post, mark out the position of the mortice slot 10in (250mm) long x the thickness of the lever post wide. The mortice slot should begin 11in (280mm) from the thinner end of the bed ⑩. Drill out the waste and then finish by cutting the mortice with a chisel ⑪ ⑫ ⑬.

In shaping the bed I kept one end wide for the seat and then tapered inwards where my legs would be positioned. This can also be done once the legs are attached and you can sit on the horse and mark exactly where your legs are and shape the horse accordingly.

⑩ Bed dimensions.

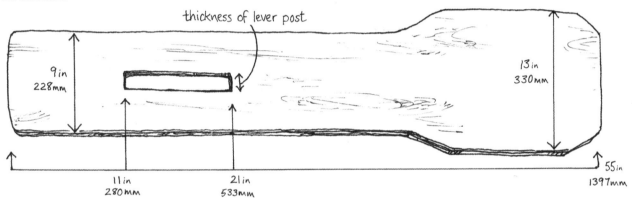

Drilling out the waste for the bed mortice.

Finishing the mortice with a framing chisel.

Checking the lever post is a good fit to the mortice.

Fixing the legs to the bed

Turn the bed upside down and mark positions for the legs. The front leg I have marked 4in (100mm) from the front edge of the bed and centrally positioned measuring across the width of the bed.

For the back legs I have measured 4in (100mm) from the back of the bed and 4in (100mm) from the sides of the bed. Using a protractor and sliding bevel, set the sliding bevel to 105 degrees for the front leg and place the sliding bevel on the bed and follow the angle with the 1in (25mm) auger as you drill out the mortice (14).

For the back legs, set the sliding bevel angle to 115 degrees and drill out the back leg mortices. It is helpful to have a second person available while you are drilling to check you are following the angle on the sliding bevel.

Insert the legs into the mortices and, using the maul, tap them through until the tenon is protruding above the top of the bed. Using the Japanese saw, rip saw a slot in the middle of the leg tenon and saw out an oak wedge (15) (16). Hammer the wedge into the slot and then saw flush with the Japanese saw (17).

Level the legs

Place the bed on a level floor and position a spirit level on the top of the bed. Chock up the legs until the bed is totally level. I use two-pence coins for this as different numbers of them can be placed under each leg until the bed is level. Using a block of wood, draw around each leg and then cut each leg to the lines you have drawn (18). The bed will now be level on its three legs (19).

Angling the auger bit in line with the sliding bevel prior to drilling the leg mortices.

Sawing out an oak wedge for the end of the leg tenon.

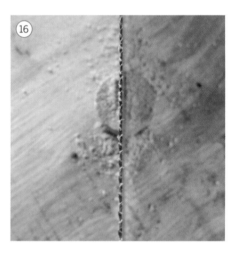

Using the Japanese saw to cut a thin slot in the end of the leg tenon.

Inserting the oak wedge into the leg tenon slot.

Drawing around the legs using a block of wood.

The level bed with attached legs.

Platform

The platform is a plank of wood that has the same width of mortice as the bed, so that the lever post can pass through both mortices. Lay the plank on top of the bed so that it covers the bed mortice and, from underneath, draw the width of the bed mortice onto the platform. The mortice in the platform does not need to be as long as the mortice in the bed – I chose 8½in (216mm) ⓳. Cut out the mortice following the same procedure as the bed mortice. Check that the lever post is a good fit through both mortices ⓴.

Saw out the platform support blocks. I have sawn these to 8 x 8in (400 x 400mm). Place the support blocks on the bed and lay the platform on top of them. The blocks should support the platform so that the edge of the platform mortice is offset from the bed mortice towards the seat end of the bed by 2in (50mm). The first platform support block I have centred 8in (200mm) from the thin end of the bed.

⓴ *Platform dimensions.*

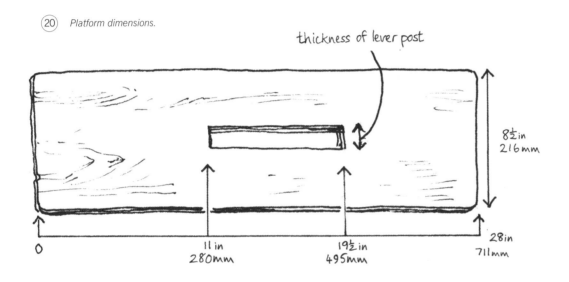

⓴

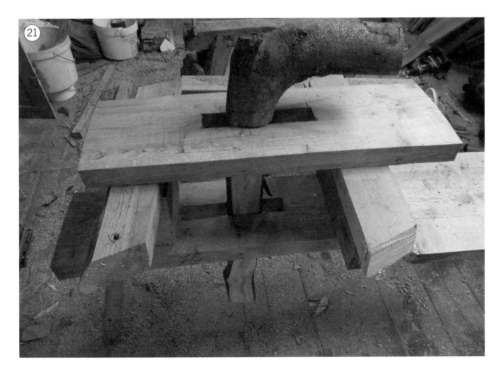

Offering the lever post to check there is a good fit through both mortices.

Add the lever post

Insert the lever post and check the positions are good before drawing around the platform support blocks to mark their position on the bed. Clamp the platform support blocks to the bed (22) and pre-drill from the underside of the bed with ¼in (6mm) auger and fix with 4in (100mm) stainless steel timber locks (23).

Lay the platform in its correct position on top of the support blocks that are now fixed to the bed (24). Check again with the lever post before fixing. Drill first with a ¾in (19mm) auger bit to the depth of about ¾in (19mm) and then complete the pre-drill using the ¼in (6mm) auger and fix with stainless steel timber locks. Plug holes with a ¾in (19mm) peg and cut flush with the Japanese saw.

Offer up the lever post and mark up for drilling the hole for the pivot peg through the platform. Drill the hole – I used a ¾in (19mm) auger bit and made an oak peg using the ¾in (19mm) rounding plane. I then took a little extra of the peg with a spoke shave to ensure the peg could be inserted and removed from the hole. Position the lever post and drill a ¾in (19mm) hole for the pivot peg. More than one hole can be drilled into the lever post to give different heights for working on different-sized pieces of wood (25).

Footplate

Saw the footplate to the dimensions shown (26). Offer up the lever post and draw lines on the foot plate. Saw down the lines marked and then drill out the waste and chisel out the mortice slot. Offer the footplate to the lever post (27) and then draw a line at the back of the lever post to know where to fit the wooden chock to hold the footplate to the lever post. I have gone for a simple solution and have let in a 1in (25mm) x 1½in (38mm) chock of oak into the footplate and then pre-drilled and fixed it with stainless steel ring shank nails (28).

Drill through the lever post with a ⅝in (15mm) auger bit below the footplate and make an oak peg of the same dimensions with the rounding plane and hammer it into position. Your shaving horse will now be ready for use (29).

Using a deep-throat clamp to secure a platform support block prior to drilling and fixing.

Fixing the platform support block to the bed using a stainless steel timber lock.

Fixing the platform support block to the bed using a stainless steel timber lock.

The lever post secured with the pivot peg.

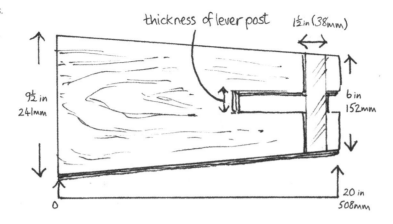

㉖ *Footplate dimensions.*

thickness of lever post

1½ in (38mm)

9½ in
241mm

6 in
152mm

0

20 in
508mm

Inserting the lever post into the footplate mortice slot.

Footplate with chock of oak inserted.

Completed Dumbhead shaving horse.

TRADITIONAL ENGLISH SHAVING HORSE

The traditional English shaving horse – sometimes referred to as a 'bodger's horse' due to its traditional use in chair making – differs from the Dumbhead and Easy Rider shaving horses as it has a separate frame built around the bed that clamps the wood as it swings on the pivot peg.

Shaving horse history

The beech woods of the Chiltern Hills was the traditional lair of the chair bodger. Through Hertfordshire, Bedfordshire, Buckinghamshire and Oxfordshire, the chalk runs in the hills and the beech tree thrives on these soils. Bodgers often lived and worked in their woods, creating large numbers of chair legs, which were later made into chairs. The bodger rarely finished a chair and the slang use of the word 'bodge' comes from a bodger doing a half-finished job. In fact, bodgers were skilled craftsmen making large numbers of chair legs with basic tools.

This bodger, in Buckinghamshire, is working on his traditional English shaving horse shaping a leg with a draw knife, prior to turning it on the pole lathe.

Materials you will need

1 log for the bed (this should give you two beds): 44in (1118mm) long and about 10½in (267mm) diameter. I used a green log of sweet chestnut, but most timbers will be fine as long as they cleave well
1 log for the frame: 30in (762mm) long and about 4in (100mm) diameter. Again, I used sweet chestnut
Seasoned oak for pegs: 50in (1270mm) long x 1½in (38mm) wide x 2in (50mm) deep
1 log for the legs: 24in (610mm) long x 5in (127mm) diameter. I used a log of sweet chestnut that had been felled three years previously
1 plank for the platform: 20in long (508mm) x 1in (25mm) deep by the width of the bed – in the case of the horse I am making, that was 6½in (165mm)
1 quartered log the width of the bed
Insulating tape

Recommended tools

Chainsaw, axe, wedges, maul, froe, cleaving brake, draw knife, side axe, drill, 1in (25mm) and ¼in (6mm) auger bits, chisel, spoke shave, clamps, Japanese saw, 1in (25mm) rounding plane, pole lathe and turning chisels (optional), sliding bevel, protractor.

① Bed dimensions.

44 in (1118mm)

6½ in
165mm

10½ in
267mm

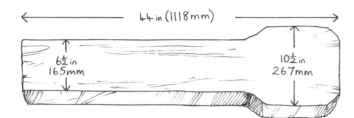

Cleaving the sweet chestnut log to make the bed.

The start of the bed.

Bed

I chose a straight stem of sweet chestnut 10½in (267mm) in diameter that I felled the previous winter and cut it to length 44in (1118mm) with the chainsaw ①. I then inserted the axe head so that it bisected the centre of the log and, hitting it with the maul, began to see the log cleave in half. I used wedges where the split had now begun to open up along the length of the log and soon the log was in two pieces ② ③.

This gave me two possible beds. I chose the one that needed less work to dress it to a level bed and then, using the chainsaw, roughly shaped the bed and seat ④. I chose a fairly narrow bed of 6½in (165mm) as most of my work on a shaving horse involves making pegs for roundwood timber framing. The size and dimensions of a shaving horse will depend on your size and shape and the type of products you are going to make on it. Next I worked the bed face to create a level bed using first the side axe and then a draw knife to take out some of the imperfections of the cleave ⑤ ⑥.

Chainsawing the bed to a workable shape and size.

Working the bed with a side axe to remove any unevenness of the cleave.

The bed levelled out.

Shape the legs

Cleave out the 24in (610mm) log into quarters and, using an axe and draw knife, shape the legs to taper towards one end (7). Use the 1in (25mm) rounding plane to create a round tenon. For the legs on this shaving horse, I did not drill the mortices right through the bed and wedge them as I have done on a number of the other projects. Instead, I drilled three-quarters of the way through the bed. Then, keeping in mind that the wood I have chosen for the legs is more seasoned than the bed (so the bed will shrink around the leg tenons), I used hidden wedges, sometimes referred to as fox wedges, to open up the tenons once the legs were inserted into the mortices.

Drill out the leg mortices

As with the other three-legged shaving horses, I angled the front leg at 105 degrees and the rear legs at 115 degrees. This is done with the sliding bevel set to the angle with the aid of a protractor. For this horse, I drilled the front leg 4in (100mm) in from the thin end of the bed and in the midpoint of the width of the bed, and the rear legs 2½in (63.5mm) in from the sides of the bed and 2½in (63.5mm) in from the rear of the bed (8). Remember, with this shaving horse, the mortices do not go right through the bed, so it can be helpful to stick a piece of insulating tape around the auger bit so that you have a depth gauge to how deep you are drilling. Use the 1in (25mm) auger bit to drill out the leg mortices.

It is helpful to have a second person with you when drilling the rear legs as the angle is not in line with the bed but closer to the line of the corner of the bed. Having a second pair of eyes to watch the angle you are drilling into the bed, as well as the auger angle in relation to the sliding bevel, can be helpful.

The chestnut log cleft into quarters. The three best will be chosen for the legs.

The sliding bevel, set at 115 degrees, acts as a guide for the auger when drilling the rear leg mortices.

Making the wedged tenon

First saw with the Japanese ripsaw down the centre of the round tenon about 1in (25mm) in depth ⑨. Using the Japanese saw again, saw out a thin tapered oak wedge of about 1in (25mm) in length. Be sure to make the wedge with the grain running down the length of the wedge, not across it. Check the wedge is slightly less wide than the round tenon and tap it gently into the saw cut you have made across the round tenon ⑩.

With the wedge sticking out of the round tenon, insert the round tenon into the leg mortice you have drilled in the bed and, as you hammer the leg in, the wedge will be pushed deeper into the tenon opening up the tenon inside the mortice to tighten the joint ⑪. Level the legs following the procedure as described for the Dumbhead shaving horse ⑫ (see page 112).

The frame sides

Take the 30in (762mm) long chestnut log and, using the froe and maul, cleave the log into two even parts ⑬ ⑭. The use of a cleaving brake can be helpful here. Clamp together the two cleft halves and, using the 1in (25mm) auger, drill out the three holes for the top jaw, pivot peg and foot rail following the frame dimensions shown in the drawing ⑮ ⑯. For the pivot peg hole you may wish to drill a second hole 2½in (63.5mm) from the first hole towards the foot rail to allow for different settings, depending upon what you are using the horse for.

Rip sawing the slot in the top of the leg tenon ready for the wedge.

The wedge inserted in the top of the leg tenon.

Inserting the hidden wedge into the mortice.

The legs now attached to the bed using the hidden wedge method.

Using the froe and cleaving brake to cleave the chestnut in two for the sides of the frame.

The two cleft halves.

(15) *Frame dimensions.*

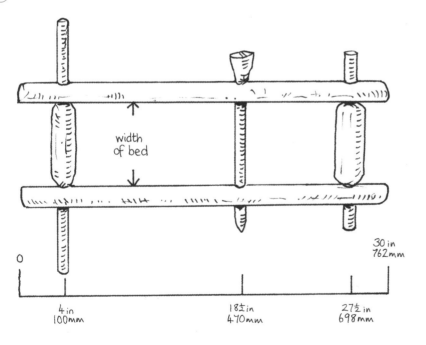

width
of bed

0

4 in
100mm

18½ in
470mm

27½ in
698mm

30 in
762mm

The frame sides clamped together in preparation for being drilled.

Top jaw, pivot peg and foot rail.

The frame attached to the bed.

Pivot peg, top jaw and foot rail

Make the pivot peg, top jaw and foot rail from the 1½in (38mm) x 2in (50mm) seasoned oak. The pivot peg I made is 14in (355mm) long and is whittled down with the draw knife. Using the 1in (25mm) rounding plane, create the peg, leaving one end fatter so that it won't pass through the 1in (25mm) hole in the frame. Use a spoke shave to make it slightly thinner (the pivot peg needs to be removable so you don't want a very tight fit).

The top jaw and foot rail are where a pole lathe can be very useful as you can turn the ends to 1in (25mm) while leaving the central part thicker so the frame is kept in square. However, if you have not yet made your pole lathe, then it can be done without one. First measure the width of your bed – my bed was 6½in (165mm) – then transfer this measurement to both the top jaw and foot rail (see drawing (15)).

For the top jaw I cut the oak to 14in (355mm) in length and for the foot rail 22in (559mm) in length. I then marked the 6½in (165mm) section in the centre of each oak blank as that is the area I won't be reducing to 1in (25mm) to fit through the holes in the cleft chestnut frame. Using the draw knife, remove surplus wood from each end of the blank. With a Japanese saw, make stop cuts where you have marked the thicker central section. These cuts are made on all sides of the blank, but not very deep, so that when using the draw knife as a push knife (working it away from you) you won't take out too much wood and affect the thicker central part.

Once you have got down to a thickness that will accept the rounding plane, round the ends down to 1in (25mm). The rounding plane leaves a taper so you will need to finish the last part up to the stop cuts using the draw knife as a push knife and a chisel. The fatter part in the middle of the top jaw can be shaped to help grip the type of items you will be shaving. I usually have one face with a right-angled edge, one slightly rounded and often cut a 'V' shape into the edge of one face for when I am whittling sawn sections of oak into pegs (17).

Pegging the top jaw and foot rail in order to stabilize the frame.

Fitting together

Drill the hole though the bed for the pivot peg using the 1in (25mm) auger. I have drilled the hole 15in (381mm) from the front of the bed and centrally though the thickness of the bed. Again, a second person can be useful here as keeping the auger bit level is important to ensure the frame sits straight when you put it all together. Now fit the frame to the bed and then drill ¼in (6mm) holes through the rounds of the top jaw and foot rail where they meet the outside of the frame and insert ¼in (6mm) pegs to keep the frame tight (18) (19).

Platform

The plank should be 20in (508mm) long x 1in (25mm) thick x the width of the bed of your horse – in this case, 6½in (165mm) (20). Choose a quartered log or split one out with an axe, for the platform support. The log should be the width of the bed so that it can be slid along the bed to vary the angle of the platform.

Clamp the platform plank to the bed with the platform support log in position (21) and drill with the 1in (25mm) auger bit at a right angle to the platform plank, through the platform plank and into the bed (22). The hole should go centrally through the platform plank and bed about 2in (50mm) from the end of the bed. Check the position of your front leg prior to drilling as you don't want to drill through that! The hole should go approximately halfway through the bed.

Create a 1in (25mm) peg from the seasoned oak about 6in (150mm) long, leaving a fat end so that the platform plank can't slide up when put under clamping pressure. Insert the peg and then drill a ¼in (6mm) hole where the platform plank and the thick end of the peg meet and insert a ¼in (6mm) peg (23). Your horse is now ready to use (24).

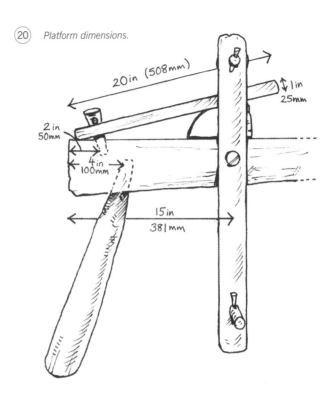

(20) *Platform dimensions.*

The platform plank and platform support log in place.

Drilling the platform plank and bed.

The platform plank secured.

The finished shave horse, ready for work.

For the platform, I used a seasoned plank of black locust (*Robinia pseudoacacia*) from my wood store. Almost any timber will do for the platform but it will be taking the force of timber clamped onto it, so I prefer to use a strong wood.

SHAVING HORSE 2000

This shaving horse was first developed by Mike Abbott. Like Sean Hellman, he has been steadily improving shaving horse design over the past twenty years. The design is based on the traditional English shaving horse but is adapted by having the platform shaped as part of the bed. This removes the play that can sometimes occur between the top jaw and the platform on the traditional English shaving horse. It is also a very compact shaving horse, easy to store or transport from place to place.

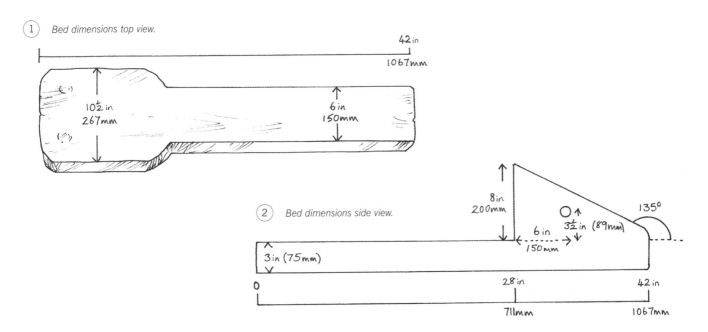

① Bed dimensions top view.

42 in
1067mm

10½ in
267mm

6 in
150mm

② Bed dimensions side view.

8 in
200mm

3½ in (89mm)

135°

6 in
150mm

3 in (75mm)

0

28 in
711mm

42 in
1067mm

③ Milling cuts for the shaving horse 2000.

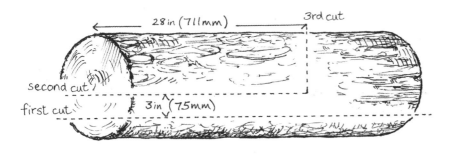

28 in (711mm)

3rd cut

second cut

first cut

3 in (75mm)

④

The freshly milled face of the black locust log will form the bed.

Materials you will need

1 log: 48in (1219mm) long x 14in (355mm) diameter. This can be made from most species of timber. Choose a durable species if the shaving horse is to live outside.

Recommended tools

Chainsaw, mobile sawmill (chainsaw can be used as a ripsaw if mobile sawmill not available), drill, 1in (25mm) and ⅜in (10mm) auger bits, 1in (25mm) rounding plane, chisel, Japanese saw, draw knife, axe, chopping block, shaving horse or vice, wedges, maul, sliding bevel, protractor, spoke shave, 1in (25mm) hollow shoulder plane, clamps.

Bed

This project needs to be made from a log as the bed and the platform need a height of 11in (280mm) – therefore a log of at least 14in (355mm) diameter is desirable. See drawings ① ② ③. First, clamp the log on the mill and make a first cut to remove the sapwood. Rotate the log through 180 degrees, so that the milled face is level on the bed ④. Do the next cut 3in (75mm) above the flat face. Stop this cut after 28in (711mm) and withdraw the sawblade.

Chainsaw down from the top of the log to meet the position where the cut with the sawmill was stopped. The large lump of waste wood that is removed during this process can be cleaved to make the other components of the shave horse.

Chainsaw the slope on the front of the platform – I find 135 degrees to be a good angle (5). Cut with the chainsaw two parallel cuts in the platform to form the sides (6). This will be where the frame attaches.

> *PLEASE ENSURE YOU ARE TRAINED IN USING A CHAINSAW AND ARE WEARING THE RELEVANT CHAINSAW SAFETY KIT (PPE) BEFORE CARRYING OUT THIS TASK.*

The bed with angled platform.

Cutting parallel sides to remove weight and ensure a vertical surface for the frame.

Selecting the wood

While choosing wood to make this shaving horse, I remembered an old log I had of black locust, which had been waiting for a use since I felled it 12 years ago. I had left it on the edge of the woodland ride and, after clearing back the brambles, I dragged it out and placed it on the sawmill. A first glance from the outside can be deceptive – most timber left out in the woodland for 12 years would be rotten and beyond use, but not black locust. I remember my friend and fellow green woodworker Mark Krawczyk, who lives in Vermont, USA, describing it as lasting 'a year longer than stone'!

I am surprised that in the British Isles we have not grown more of this durable timber. There seems to be a concern that because it suckers freely it could become invasive. While I understand these concerns, I believe that a timber that is as at least as durable as oak would be harvested and managed and therefore any invasive tendencies controlled. It also has other advantages, such as it has the ability to fix nitrogen and it is a good nectar tree for bees.

The deceptive look of the black locust log.

Cleaving out the black locust for the legs and frame.

Using the sliding bevel as an angle guide for drilling out the front leg.

Using the rounding plane to create the round leg tenon.

Shaping the legs

Cleave out three legs and, using the axe and a chopping block, roughly shape the legs (7). I have made the legs 24in (610mm) long – this allows for a 3in (75mm) round tenon to go through the bed. Draw knife the legs to a finish and, using the 1in (25mm) rounding plane, create the tenons on each leg (8). For more detail on making each leg, please refer to making the legs on the Dumbhead shaving horse (see page 109).

Drilling out the legs

With the legs made, turn the bed upside down and, using a protractor, set the sliding bevel to 105 degrees and position it so that it can be used as a guide for drilling the front leg mortice (9). Using the 1in (25mm) auger bit drill the front mortice in the midpoint of the width of the bed and 4½in (114mm) from the front of the bed.

Set the sliding bevel to 115 degrees and drill out the back leg mortices 2½in (64mm) from the back and 2½in (64mm) from the side of the bed. This is a compound angle so make sure the auger bit is angled at 115 degrees in line with the corner of the bed, so that the legs angle outwards.

Wedging the legs

Hammer the leg tenons into the mortices and, using the Japanese saw, cut a thin wedge and make a saw cut in the top of the leg tenon, which should be slightly proud of the bed surface. Hammer the wedge home to secure the leg and then cut flush to the surface of the bed with the Japanese saw (10). Level the legs of the shaving horse, following the description of levelling the legs on the Dumbhead shaving horse (see page 112) (11).

The top of the wedged leg as seen from the top of the bed, having been flush cut with the Japanese saw.

The bed with shaped platform and legs.

Frame

Cleave out two pieces to create the sides of the frame that, when finished, should measure 30in (762mm) long and 3in (75mm) wide by 1½in (38mm) deep (12). Using an axe and a draw knife, work the wood to create a matching pair of sides. Clamp the two sides together and mark the positions for drilling out for the top jaw, pivot peg and footrest peg and now drill it with a 1in (25mm) auger bit (13). You may choose to have more than one position for the pivot peg but the measurements shown are a good guide for your first set up.

Pivot peg

Using the rounding plane, create a 1in (25mm) peg, 16in (406mm) long for the pivot peg. Leave the end 1½in (38mm) fatter than the rest of the peg. Using a spoke shave, take a little more of the peg so that it is not too tight as this peg will need to be removed if you change the height or position of the frame (14).

Top jaw

This should also be 16in (406mm) long but only 4½in (114mm) at each end of the peg should be taken down to 1in (25mm) diameter, leaving the middle 7in (178mm) thicker to grip the pieces of wood you will be using with the shaving horse. I like to leave this middle section of the top jaw with at least one flat face on it and I often cut out a 'V' section in another of the faces to give me different gripping options – the rough chainsawed face on the platform also helps with this.

To make the 1in (25mm) round ends you can use a hollow shoulder plane – this differs from a rounding plane as it leaves a defined shoulder between the round part exiting the plane and the blank of wood you are making it from, whereas a rounding plane leaves a taper between the two (15). If you don't have a hollow shoulder plane, then use the rounding plane to get as far as you can from each end and then use a Japanese saw to carefully saw where the rounds meet the middle section and then chisel to these cuts, removing the tapered wood left by the rounding plane.

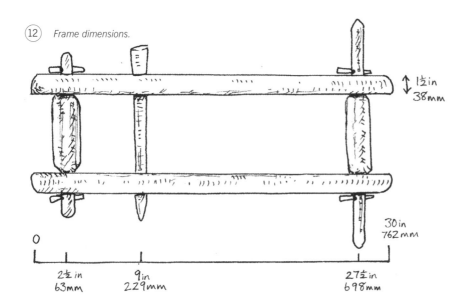

(12) Frame dimensions.

↕ 1½in 38mm

30in 762mm

0

2½in 63mm

9in 229mm

27½in 698mm

Drilling through the sides of the frame.

FAR LEFT: From top to bottom: top jaw, pivot peg and foot peg.

LEFT: A hollow shoulder plane.

Frame attached to bed.

Peg holding the frame together.

Breaking in the horse.

Foot peg

The process for this is the same as the top jaw except the two end sections extend out so that your feet can control the frame. I used a 22in (559mm) length, with a 7in (178mm) long thicker central section and a 7¹/₂in (190mm) length of 1in (25mm) peg left at each end. Next you need to drill out a 1in (25mm) hole through the platform to receive the pivot peg. I created a hole 6in (150mm) from the right-angled edge of the platform and 3¹/₂in (89mm) up from the top of the bed. You can drill other holes through the platform to vary the position of the frame on the bed.

Assemble the frame with the bed by hammering the pivot peg through the hole you have drilled though the platform (16). Make four ³/₈in (10mm) diameter pegs, 2in (50mm) long, pre-drilling the top jaw and the foot peg on the outside of where they meet the frame. Hammer in the pegs to secure the frame (17). Your shaving horse is now complete (18) (19).

The completed shaving horse.

Draw knifing a chestnut billet on the shaving horse 2000 amongst the coppice regeneration of the previous winter's cut.

BRAKES

Brakes are a group of devices, the main purpose of which is to hold a piece of wood while the craftsperson cleaves the wood into smaller pieces. The brake not only grips the wood but allows the craftsperson to exert pressure onto one part of the wood to control or correct the direction of the cleave. Brakes are used in any craft where wood is split but are most commonly used for pales, rails, shakes and laths.

SHAKE BRAKE

The shake brake is a simple device, the origins of which I believe come from Bulgaria. It comprises a large beam into which a number of different-sized angled slots are cut. As you cleave your log into smaller sections, the brake both holds the wood while you cleave the shake but also allows pressure to be put onto the cleave to straighten it, if it is running out. As someone who has made a lot of shakes, I find this device a great asset.

Materials you will need

1 beam (or log to create a beam from):
51in (1295mm) long x 6in (150mm) wide
x 8in (200mm) deep
2 trestles
2 ratchet straps

Recommended tools

Chainsaw, protractor, sliding bevel,
carpenter's square, framing chisel, froe
and maul for making shakes.

Finished shakes in the workshop. Note the draw-knifed bevel on the end grain.

Selecting wood

First select your beam. The dimensions I am using are just
a guide ①. I had surplus timber left from the black locust
log I used to make the shaving horse 2000 (see page 126) and
therefore utilized the size available. The beam needs to be
strong and preferably not made from a timber that is prone
to cleaving (so, for once, I would avoid sweet chestnut). I have
made good shake brakes from oak in the past.

Legs or no legs

I have avoided fixing legs to the brake (although this
can be done) as the brake is easier to transport and
store as one piece. This also allows for it to be set up
at whatever height the shake maker chooses. I have
attached mine to two carpenter's trestles, so if you
haven't already made a pair of trestles, perhaps now
is the time to attempt that project (see page 154).

① *Shake brake dimensions.*

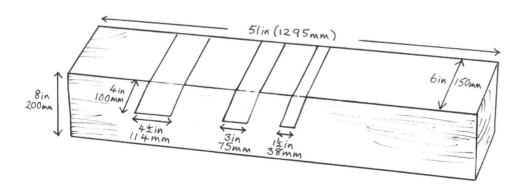

The waste pieces from cleaving shakes in the process of being transformed to kindling.

Securing and marking the beam

Secure the brake beam to the trestles using a couple of ratchet straps (2). Using the protractor, set the sliding bevel to 65 degrees. Mark the 65-degree angle on the beam, coming down 4in (100mm) from the top of the beam (3). Using the carpenter's square, take the line across the top of the beam (4). Take the line down the other side using the sliding bevel and finish the line 4in (100mm) from the top.

Notching the beam

How many notches you cut out of the log and how wide they are will depend on the size of round log you are cleaving your shakes from. I utilize sweet chestnut of mainly between 7 and 10in (175 to 250mm) and the shake brake dimensions drawing shown is based on this. But you will need a sequence of notches going from large to small. Make sure to leave enough wood attached to the original log between the notches, as there will be pressure put on those areas in the cleaving process.

Use a chainsaw to follow the lines you have marked and then plunge cut through the log to remove the waste (5). A plunge cut takes practice so it may be worth trying this out on a less valuable piece of wood before plunging into your beam. A carving bar on the chainsaw can give you more control. Repeat the practice for the other notches. For the thinnest notch, the chainsaw bar will be too wide to plunge cut, so this can either be removed with a framing chisel or by carrying out a number of vertical chainsaw cuts next to each other (6). The shake brake is now ready to work (7).

The beam secured to two trestles with ratchet straps.

Marking the angle for the chainsaw cuts with the sliding bevel.

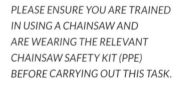

PLEASE ENSURE YOU ARE TRAINED IN USING A CHAINSAW AND ARE WEARING THE RELEVANT CHAINSAW SAFETY KIT (PPE) BEFORE CARRYING OUT THIS TASK.

Taking the line over the top of the beam using the carpenter's square.

Plunge cutting with the chainsaw.

A completed notch.

Shake brake ready for work.

Using the shake brake

Take your round log and cleave it in two with the froe. Offer the half log into the largest of the notches and, using the froe, split off a shake or two. As the log gets smaller, move to a smaller notch. Continue the process until you have split out all the log. If the cleave starts to run off, put your hand in the cleave behind the froe and exert side pressure on the shake while it is gripped in the brake.

Using the brake notches to cleave out the shakes.

Splitting out the log.

Cleaving using the thinnest notch.

The chestnut shake roofs of the Gateway Buildings at the Weald and Downland Museum, Sussex, UK. They feature 60,000 shakes made by the author and Justin Owen.

CLEAVING BRAKE

Designed to assist with the cleaving or riving of wood, the two horizontal poles that form the brake allow controlled leverage to the wood you are working. I use them for cleaving posts, pales, laths and small-diameter weaving material. The dimensions of the brake will depend on your build and the materials you are cleaving.

Materials you will need

2 poles: 78in (1981mm) long x 5in (125mm) diameter
2 poles: 60in (1524mm) long x 4in (100mm) diameter
A few poles for bracing: 48in (1219mm) long x 4in (100mm) diameter. These poles are often added over time as the constant use of the brake begins to make the main legs a bit wobbly. I have chosen sweet chestnut for the construction as its durability in the ground will give me a good few years of service.
Timber locks or coach screws: 6in (150mm)

Recommended tools

Post rammer, chainsaw, panel saw, axe, chisel, ¼in (6mm) auger bit, drill, impact driver, maul and froe for cleaving.

PLEASE ENSURE YOU ARE TRAINED IN USING A CHAINSAW AND ARE WEARING THE RELEVANT CHAINSAW SAFETY KIT (PPE) BEFORE CARRYING OUT THIS TASK.

Legs

Point the two legs and hammer into the ground using the post rammer ①. The posts should be about 50in (1270mm) apart from each other ②.

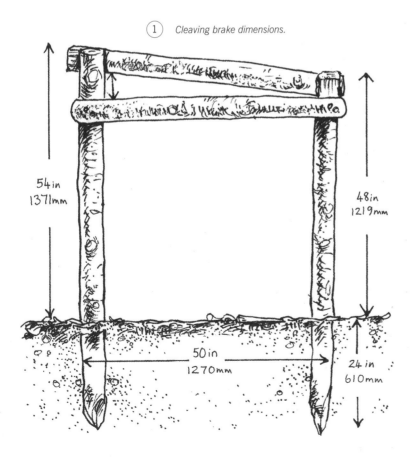

① *Cleaving brake dimensions.*

54in 1371mm

48in 1219mm

50in 1270mm

24in 610mm

Using the post rammer to sink the legs.

With an extra person if possible, offer up the horizontal poles to the legs and mark where they will overlap the legs. Using the panel saw, make shallow cuts and then chisel out where you have marked the overlaps ③. Repeat this process on the horizontal poles. You should now have flats on both the legs and horizontal poles ④.

Offer the poles to the legs

First check you have good surface contact between the flats. Make any adjustments as necessary. Pre-drill through the horizontal poles with the ¼in (6mm) auger and fix with timber locks using the impact driver. Use two fixings in each joint, fixed at a slightly skewed angle for strength ⑤.

Fix the level horizontal pole first and then adjust the angled horizontal pole to get the distance between the poles that you need for the work you are doing. I have set mine to run from 0 to 5in (125mm) ⑥. The support braces can be fitted over time as and when the brake needs stabilizing ⑦. The cleave brake is now ready to use.

Flat face created on the leg.

Chiselling out a flat face on the end of one of the horizontal poles.

Skew fixing the horizontal pole to the leg.

The completed cleaving brake.

Optional support braces.

Cleaving with the brake.

How to use a cleaving brake

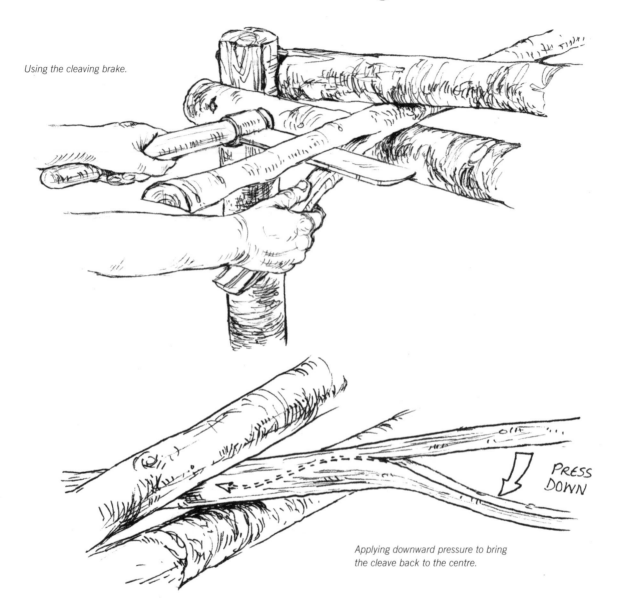

Using the cleaving brake.

Applying downward pressure to bring the cleave back to the centre.

PRESS DOWN

Insert the round of wood to be cleaved into the brake and slide it across the brake so that it grips. Using the maul and froe, knock the froe into the end grain of the log, making sure to pass right through the centre of the log. The froe should now begin to open up a split in the round of wood.

By levering the froe handle from side to side, while pushing the froe deeper into the log, the cleave will work its way through the log. If the cleave starts to run out, put the thicker end of the split facing downwards in the brake and push down on the thicker side. This will bring the cleave back into the centre of the log.

A temporary cleaving brake set up in the woods for chestnut posts.

An old cleaving brake lies dormant in the coppice re-growth.

TRIANGULATED CLEAVING BRAKE

The triangulated cleaving brake is a sturdy cleaving brake with two cleft faces opposing each other to form the brake. The flat cleft faces and the wider distance apart of the poles make this cleaving brake ideal for making laths.

Materials you will need

1 log: 68in (1727mm) long x 8in (200mm) diameter
2 logs: 57in (1447mm) long x 6in (150mm) diameter
1 log: 62in (1575mm) long x 6in (150mm) diameter
1 log: 42in (1066mm) long x 4½in (114mm) diameter
Timber locks: 8in (200mm)

I made the illustrated brake from sweet chestnut, but any wood that cleaves well could be used.

Recommended tools

Post rammer, panel saw, framing chisel, maul, drill, impact driver, ¼in (6mm) auger bit, axe, wedges.

Making the posts and cleaved pieces

Point the three posts with an axe and, using the post rammer, hammer the first two posts into the ground 62in (1575mm) apart, leaving 33in (838mm) above ground ①.

Using first the axe head and then the wedges, cleave the 68in (1727mm) long pole ② ③. With the panel saw, framing chisel and maul, create two parallel flat faces on the uncleaved side of one of the cleaved pieces, removing about 1in (25mm) so that when it sits on top of the two posts the cleaved face will be approximately 36in (914mm) from the ground ④.

① Triangulated cleaving brake dimensions.

60in 1524mm
36in 914mm
62in (1575mm)
36in 914mm
33in 838mm
24in 610mm

②

Cleaving out the 8in (200mm) diameter log using axe head and wedges.

③ ④

FAR LEFT: Two cleaved faces that form the brake.

LEFT: Creating a flat on one end of the log to ensure good contact with the post.

Fixing together

Pre-drill with the ¼in (6mm) auger and, using the impact driver, fix with two 6in (150mm) timber locks through the cleaved face at each end into the posts ⑤. Knock in the third post and then offer the other cleaved half to the third post, cleaved face down, making sure it raises up approximately 5in (125mm) from the height of the first cleaved half ⑥.

Pre-drill and fix with timber locks. Offer up the shorter round pole to complete the triangle. Flatten the ends to ensure a good contact and then pre-drill and fix. The triangulated cleaving brake is now ready for use ⑦.

Using this cleaving brake

The triangulated cleaving brake gives more control and support than the standard cleaving brake and I favour it where I have a large order of small-diameter material to cleave such as laths or for cleaving small diameter chestnut or hazel for woven panels.

The first cleaved piece fixed to the posts.

The second cleaved piece fixed in place.

The completed triangulated cleaving bed.

Making laths on the triangulated cleaving brake.

Cleaving small diameter sweet chestnut rods for woven panels on the triangulated cleaving brake.

WOODLAND AND WORKSHOP DEVICES

This chapter brings together a selection of useful devices that are of great assistance when making woodland craft produce. Some of these devices, such as the framing bed, need a large amount of space and are more likely to be set up in the woods with the possibility of a temporary workshop constructed over them. Others, such as the trestle and chopping block, are likely to find a permanent place within the workshop as they are such useful devices you will wonder how you ever managed without them!

CARPENTER'S TRESTLE

The carpenter's trestle has been used for hundreds of years to raise work to a comfortable height. When used as a pair, trestles can be used as an aid for sawing timber or for more complicated tasks such as the laying out of a timber-framed building. This trestle is not the most simple to construct and has a few challenging angles to cut, but it is a model I have been using for over twenty years and has stood the test of time as a robust trestle that won't let you down.

Cutting a peg blank using a trestle and a Japanese saw.

Materials you will need

I recommend Douglas fir for the majority of trestles but I have used oak when making trestles for timber framing.

1 length of sawn timber for the bed: 36in (900mm) long x 4in (100mm) wide x 4in (100mm) wide
4 lengths of sawn timber for the legs: 26in (660mm) long x 4in (100mm) wide x 2in (50mm) deep
2 lengths of sawn timber for the bracing: 12in (300mm) long x 4in (100mm) wide x 2in (50mm) deep
Timber screws: 8 x 2½in (65mm), 8 x 4in (100mm)

Recommended tools

Panel saw, Japanese rip saw, carpenter's square, vice or clamp to hold the wood, protractor, sliding bevel, drill, screwdriver or impact driver.

The foot of the legs

Using the carpenter's square and panel saw, saw one end of each leg square ①. Set the sliding bevel to 60 degrees by using the protractor to set the angle ②. Draw 60-degree angle on the leg from where you have cut it square. Mark these points A and C as on drawing ③.

Using the carpenter's square, draw a line from point A to find point B. Saw the end of the timber from points C to A to B ④. The fourth corner of this cut will be point D. Measure 23 5/16in (592mm) from point A to find point E. Measure 23 5/16in (592mm) from point C to find point D. Measure 24in (610mm) from point B to find point F (again, refer to drawing ③). Saw the angle from point D to B to F in one cut. This will create the foot of the leg.

Using the carpenter's square to draw a line square on each leg.

Using the protractor to set the sliding bevel to 60 degrees.

③   *Initial layout for the leg.*

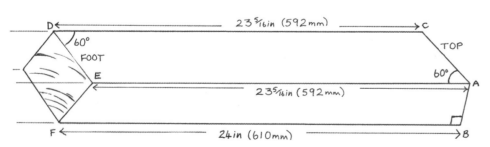

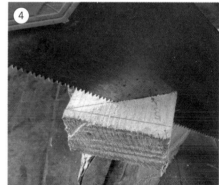

Sawing points C to A to B.

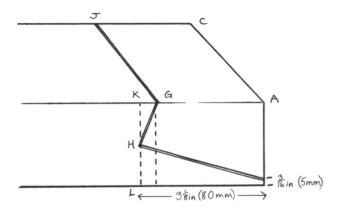

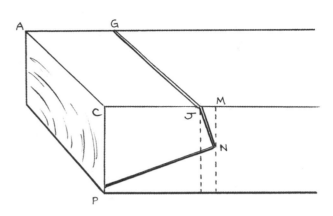

(5) *Reference points to mark and cut the legs.*

(6) *Further reference points to mark and cut the legs.*

Marking the leg angles

Measure 2¾in (70mm) from point A to find point G and draw a 90-degree line with the carpenter's square – see drawing (5). Measure 3⅛in (80mm) from point A to find point K. Using the carpenter's square, draw a 90-degree line from point K to find point L.

Measure up 1in (25mm) from point L to find point H. This is the midpoint between point L and point K. Draw a line from point H to point G. Measure up ³/16in (5mm) from point B and draw a line from this point back to point H. The angle from this new point to point H to point G should be a right angle (90 degrees). Using the sliding bevel (still set at 60 degrees), draw a line from point G to new point J. This line should be parallel to point A to point C. Your markings should now look as shown in drawing (5).

Mark up the opposite side. Using the carpenter's square draw a 90-degree line down from point J. Measure ³/8in (10mm) towards the foot of the leg from point J to find point M. Draw a 90-degree line down from point M with the carpenter's square. Measure down 1in (25mm) from point M to find point N and draw a line from point N to point J. Measure up ³/16in (5mm) from point P and draw a line from this point to point N (6).

Cutting the leg angles

Saw the angle from points N to J to G to H as one cut (7). Saw the angle line from the points ³/16in (5mm) above points P and B to meet points N and H. This is a tricky cut as you are rip sawing and starting at a point ³/16in (5mm) in from the edge of the wood. I use a Japanese ripsaw for this as the blade is very fine and gives a good clean cut (8).

The angle cut from points N to J to G to H.

Rip sawing with the Japanese saw.

Finished cuts showing leg ready to fit to the bed.

Finishing the legs

Now repeat the process of marking and cutting the angles for the next leg, using the first leg as a template ⑨. For the other two legs, the process is the same except they need to be the mirror image of the first two legs ⑩.

The bed

Using the carpenter's square, mark and then saw the 4 x 4in (100 x 100mm) piece of timber to 36in (914mm) in length.

Assembly

Measure 5in (125mm) in from each end of the bed and make a 90-degree pencil line with the carpenter's square on each side of the bed. Offer the leading edge (this will be your original point B) to meet the pencil line and pre-drill and fix. I have used a ¼in (6mm) drill bit to pre-drill through the leg and then used an impact driver and 2½in (65mm) hex-head timber screw to secure the legs to the bed – two screws in each leg ⑪.

The bracing must be fixed across each pair of legs. With the trestle standing on the workshop floor, measure up 12in (300mm) from the floor and mark each leg at that height with a pencil. Offer the braces across each pair of legs, so that the lowest point of the brace meets the pencil marks and sits 12in (300mm) from the workshop floor. Pre-drill and screw. I used 4in (100mm) hex-headed timber screws (four in each brace) ⑫. Saw off any surplus wood sticking out from where the braces are fixed to the legs and your trestle is ready for work ⑬.

The mirror image for the opposing pair of legs.

Screwing the legs to the bed.

Braces screwed to the legs.

The completed trestle.

Apprentice work

It has been a tradition in many cultures that making trestles is an early job for a carpenter's apprentice. It is an opportunity for the apprentice to show their accuracy in sawing and jointing and to practise skills on a piece that is not commissioned from their master.

Adapting trestles

The trestle has so many uses and adaptabilities and plays an important part in the woodland workshop. A pair of trestles with the addition of a clamp becomes a vice, with a plank they become a scaffold. As I work a lot with round poles, I often attach a couple of wooden blocks to the top of a trestle. These have an angled cut and are fixed with one long timber screw. They are fixed securely but not too tight as they need to be manually twisted to tighten against the diameter of the pole inserted between them.

A well-used trestle showing the addition of angled wooden blocks for gripping round poles.

Pair of trestles being used for morticing a post.

WORKSHOP
CHOPPING BLOCK

A solid but portable chopping block is an essential part of my workshop set-up. Many items I make involve shaping wood with a side axe to create a rough billet before more detailed draw knifing. This is a quick project that produces a useful workshop item and will give you many years of use.

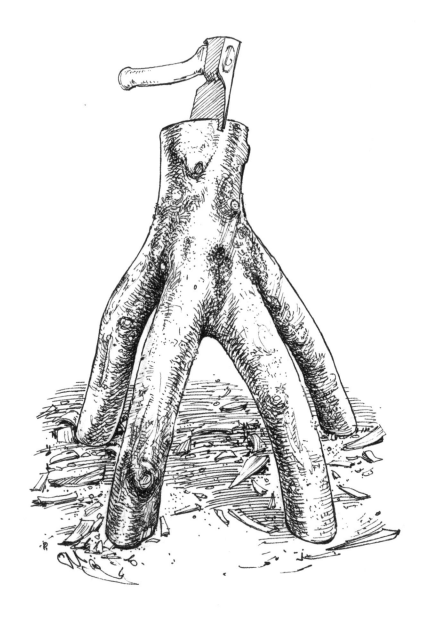

Shaping a stool leg on the workshop chopping block.

Materials you will need

1 branched lead stem of a tree – species not important.

Recommended tools

Chainsaw (or handsaw or axe) for felling the tree, spirit level, panel saw.

My chosen tree with a good spread of branches.

Seeing products in the trees

While I am out cutting coppice in the winter months, I am always looking for products in the trees. Being able to see a product at an early stage while felling coppice is one of the skills of being a woodsman. For a chopping block, I look for a sturdy tree that has lost the main lead stem and has evenly branched out with three or four sturdy branches. These branches will eventually form the legs of the chopping block. The tree must then be carefully felled to ensure the branches do not split or break on impact.

Choosing your tree

If you are felling coppice you will be felling a good-sized area and should not only have a choice of suitable trees but you will avoid the difficulty of felling one particular tree that is growing in amongst many others. Look for branches of even thickness that are spreading out from the tree but still growing upwards for the light.

Grey squirrels and tree branching

Generally, grey squirrels cause more damage to trees than any other creature in the British Isles and should be controlled and not encouraged.

However, when it comes to finding wood for a chopping block, this is one of the very few times that I feel the grey squirrel has helped the woodsman. Grey squirrels cause a huge amount of damage to commercial timber by removing the bark all the way around the circumference of the tree. They do this to gain material for creating their dreys (nests of bark and leaves) and to feed on the sugars flowing in the tree sap.

Once they have ring barked the circumference of the tree, the flow of sap is cut off and the tree dies off above this point, but sometimes will send out multiple stems, which create the legs of the chopping block.

Wood block size

Once the tree is felled, you will be able to examine the potential chopping block (1). I like to end up with a chopping block of approximately 32in (813mm) from the ground to chopping surface. This size will depend on how tall you are and what you find a comfortable height to work at.

Cut off the tree from its main stem and then cut each branch individually, leaving them all longer than your desired finished size. The chopping block surface will be strong and difficult to split (which is important) as the grain of the wood will be changing direction and growing out into the individual legs.

Take the chopping block back to your workshop (or anywhere you have a level floor), and stand the block up with a spirit level on the chopping surface. Using wood offcuts or cardboard, place pieces under each leg until the chopping block is upright and the spirit level shows the chopping surface is level (2). Measure down from the chopping surface to the ground. Calculate the difference between the measured height and the finished height you are looking for.

With that measurement, find a block of wood of that height and, placing it at each leg, draw all the way around the legs (3). Cut the legs off following the pencil lines, stand the chopping block up again and you will have a level chopping block at your chosen working height.

The felled tree with my chopping block beginning to appear.

Drawing around the legs using a chosen size of block.

Levelling the chopping block.

FRAMING BED

If there is one woodland device that has helped form my direction in life, it would have to be the framing bed. The framing bed has helped create my house, workshop and many other buildings and has been at the heart of the roundwood timber-frame building movement. It is a simple device to construct, provided you have the space to build it.

Benefits of the framing bed

The framing bed has been the catalyst for overcoming so many of the natural intricacies and characteristics that a natural roundwood pole contains. It has enabled me to not only work with those shapes but translate them into an order that creates buildings and forms that have a logic and allow mathematical calculation.

A frame laid out on a framing bed.

Materials you will need

For a permanent bed:
6 lengths of sawn timber: 197in (5000mm) long x 6in (150mm) wide x 4in (100mm) deep
9 round poles (chestnut recommended): 54in (1371mm) long x 7in (175mm) diameter

For a temporary bed:
12 lengths of sawn timber: 197in (5000mm) long x 6in (150mm) wide x 2in (50mm) deep
9 round poles (any timber): 54in (1371mm) long x 7in (175mm) diameter
Timber locks and screws

Recommended tools

Tamper, spade, 3/4/5 triangle, drill, impact driver, screws, timber locks, saw, chisel, maul, spirit level, laser, tripod. A post-hold auger is also useful.

Sizing

If you are building a permanent framing bed, which will be used for the construction of many different frames, then I recommend 6 x 4in (150 x 100mm) timbers. If, however, you are making a temporary bed for the construction of one building, I recommend making the bed from pairs of 6 x 2in (150 x 50mm) timbers joined together, which, once the frames have been built on the bed, can be taken apart and reused as the floor joists in the building.

The lengths of timber for this project are for a generic framing bed, but always make the bed wide enough to carry frames the width of your proposed building.

Positioning the posts

Using the 3/4/5 triangle, mark out the positions of the posts in a grid pattern. I have made each post 88in (2235mm) from the next one (1). Dig the holes by spade or auger to a depth of 24in (600mm). Do not point the posts and use a post rammer – they need to sit flat in the base of the holes. If they were pointed, the weight of timbers on top of the bed could push a post slightly further into the ground and, in doing so, throw the whole framing bed out of level.

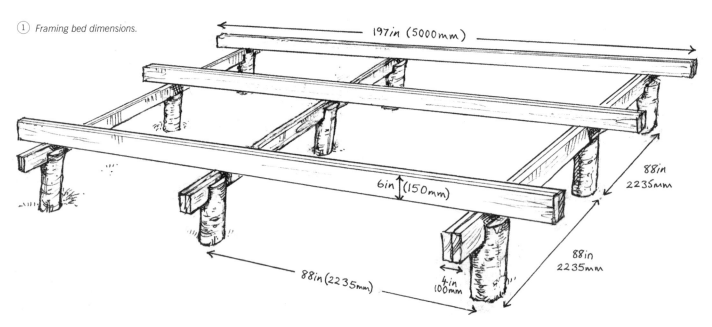

① *Framing bed dimensions.*

Back fill the holes and use the tamper to firm the posts up. Set up the laser level on a tripod to your chosen height ②. I set the tripod so the laser marked the first post at 18in (450mm) above the ground and then marked where the laser line crossed each of the posts.

Remember, your finished working height will be 12in (300mm) above the laser mark, so I will end up with a working height of 30in (762mm) above the ground. If your ground is sloping, you will end up with a varied working height across the bed. It is tempting to build the bed higher but remember the higher the bed, the higher it will be to lift the poles onto the bed!

Saw the top off each post about 4in (100mm) above the level mark, then saw at the level mark a cut of about 4 to 5in (100 to 125mm) in depth. Chisel down from the top of the post to leave a ledge for the timbers to sit on.

A laser and tripod for marking the levels on the posts.

Alternative to a laser

If you don't have access to a laser, you could always make a 'bunyip' water level and use that instead. You will need two 48in (1219mm) lengths of wood 3in (75mm) x 1in (25mm) and 192in (4877mm) of ½in (12mm) clear plastic water pipe and four large jubilee clips or strong clear tape. Mark a matching scale (imperial, metric or both) onto each piece of wood and tape each end of the plastic pipe to the wood. Holding both pieces of wood upright, fill with water until the water is halfway up each scale.

Working with a second person, get them to hold one piece of wood upright by your first post, while you walk with the second upright piece of wood with your thumb over the top of the plastic pipe and not lifting it too high to the second post, remove your thumb and the water will find its natural level. Continue this process using the scales on the wood to mark each post. Water is a very accurate levelling medium.

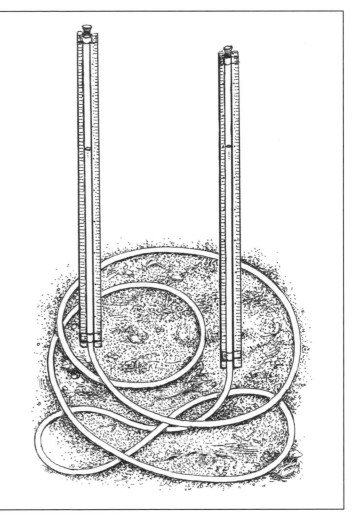

Bunyip water level.

Using the 3/4/5 triangle to get the layers of the framing bed at 90 degrees.

Positioning the timbers

If you are making a temporary framing bed, screw the 6 x 2in (150 x 50mm) timbers together, making sure they will be easy to undo again. Next, position the timbers on the ledge you have created on the posts, line them up and check they are level before pre-drilling and fixing them with timber locks.

Place the next layer of timbers on top, making sure they are lined up over the top of the posts – use the 3/4/5 triangle to make sure they are at 90 degrees to the lower layer of timbers ③. This is very important as it will affect the layout of your frames. Check the top layer is level and pre-drill and fix with timber locks. Your framing bed is now ready for use ④.

The completed framing bed.

Using the framing bed

The framing bed is a level map upon which you layout your roundwood frames. By marking positions of components of a frame on the bed, you can remove them, replace them with other timbers and get a mirror image frame. Because the framing bed is horizontally level, making the frames on it will ensure they stand up vertical. The bed can be used as a reference – it is possible to measure up at any point from the bed to your roundwood frame and calculate the difference in height. The right-angled nature of the framing bed allows you to lay out round poles parallel to the timbers of the framing bed and use the timbers that run at 90 degrees to help mark out floor beams and tie beams with confidence .

If you are using a framing bed for making multiple frames of different sizes, think carefully about how you mark the bed. Pencil lines are fine for your first project but multiple pencil lines can lead to error so consider using different colours for each project. If it is wet, use indelible pencils as they will write better when the wood is wet.

Students working on a frame during one of my roundwood timber-framing courses.

My roundwood timber-frame house, constructed on a framing bed and raised by hand in the woods.

BUNDLERS

This simple device is often used together with the woodsman's grip (see page 176) for bundling produce such as bean poles, faggots or pales. Bundling is very important when making pales – they must be stored in very tight bundles prior to being made into fencing rolls or the greenwood can bend and distort.

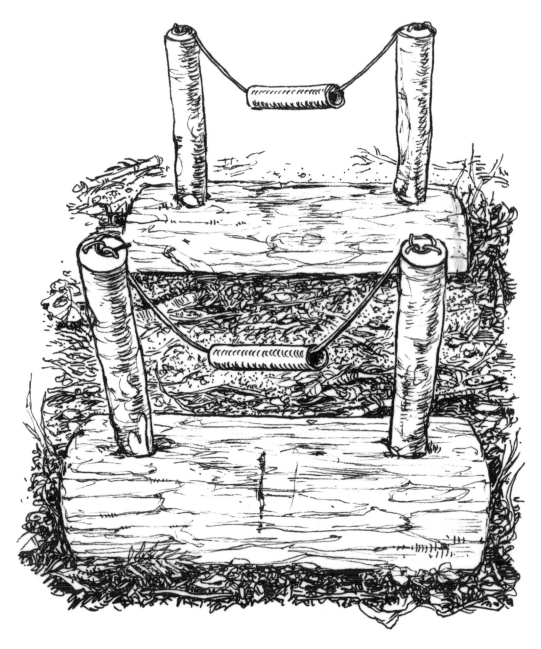

Materials you will need (per bundler)

1 piece of slab wood or large plank: 24in (600mm) long
x 11in (279mm) wide by 4in (100mm) deep
2 poles: 18in (450mm) long x 2in (50mm) diameter
1 bucket handle or thick wire
4 fencing staples

Recommended tools

1½in (38mm) bar auger, axe, saw, hammer.

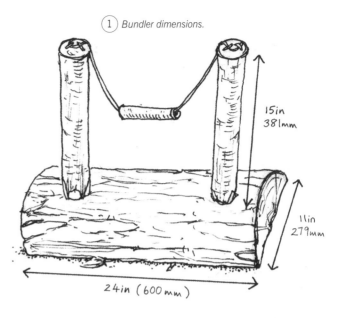

1 *Bundler dimensions.*

15in
381mm

11in
279mm

24in (600mm)

Using the bar auger to drill holes in the slab wood.

Constructing the bundler

Using the 1½in (38mm) bar auger, drill two holes into the centre of the slab wood 16in (406mm) apart and 2½in (64mm) deep 1 2. Use the axe to shave down the ends of the poles so that they fit tightly into the holes and hammer home 3. Bend the tops of the bucket handle so that they fit flat onto the tops of the poles and secure with two fencing staples into each pole 4.

Axing the ends of the poles to get a snug fit in the holes.

A completed bundler.

Bundling up the last of the season's hazel bean poles.

The finished bundle.

WOODSMAN'S GRIP

The woodsman's grip is a device used to tighten a pile of material, often brash, into a tight bundle. The woodsman's grip traditionally uses a fibre rope but I have adapted it to use a wire rope and a clamp as the clamp makes easy adjustment for the length of the wire rope between the lever handles. This is particularly useful when bundling faggots where you are aiming for a particular diameter bundle of brash.

Woodsman's grip history

Many craft products such as spars and pales need to be bundled very tightly, not just because if they are loose, they may fall out of the bundle when being thrown up onto a lorry or wagon, but because keeping them tight keeps them straight and avoids them distorting as they dry out. With spars, a tight bundle reduces the air flow around each individual spar and helps maintain moisture, keeping them flexible for the thatcher to use.

A woodsman's grip being used to bundle up thatching spars, Ebernoe, 1939. Note the Sussex knee vice in the background.

Materials you will need

2 poles: 34in (864mm) long x 2in (50mm) diameter
Wire rope: 52in (1320mm) long x ¼in (6mm) diameter
2 wire rope clamps: ¼in (6mm)

Recommended tools

Saw, drill, ³⁄₈in (10mm) auger bit, pliers.

Woodsman origins

The use of the word 'man' in 'woodsman' is not a reference to gender, as men and women are equally capable of woodland work. It comes from 'manus', the Latin word meaning 'hand'. Thus, woodsman refers to 'hand of the woods'.

Making the grip

Drill a hole 6in (150mm) from the end of each pole using the ³⁄₈in (10mm) auger bit ① ②. The hole can be further from the end of the pole if you want longer ends to your poles to increase leverage. Thread the ¼in (6mm) wire rope through the holes and, using the pliers, tighten the clamps so that you have your chosen length of wire rope between the poles ③. The grip is now ready to use ④.

② *Woodsman's grip dimensions.*

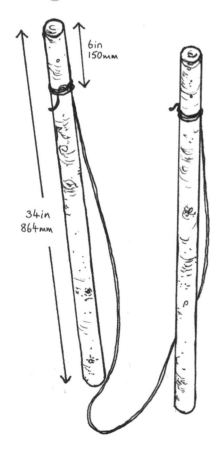

6in
150mm

34in
864mm

The holes drilled through the poles, ready to receive the wire rope.

The tightened clamp, ensuring the wire rope cannot slip back through the holes.

The completed woodsman's grip.

The woodsman's grip and bundlers in use.

Using the woodsman's grip and bundlers

The woodsman's grip is usually used with the bundlers to tighten bundles prior to tying. With your product laying in the bundlers, loop the wire rope around the bundle and, by pushing the poles apart, the bundle will tighten.

By sitting astride the bundle, once the bundle is under tension from the woodsman's grip, you can use your knees to hold the poles in position, freeing up your hands to tie the bundle.

POLE LATHE

The pole lathe and its associates, the spring and treadle lathes, were used to turn bowls and were the mainstay of the bodger's trade in turning chair legs. Still used today by traditional greenwood chair makers, this beautiful low-technology device can bring many hours of therapeutic activity.

Materials you will need

2 lengths of sawn timber for the bed:
60in (1524mm) long x 4¾in (121mm) wide x 1¾in (44mm) deep
1 length of timber for the poppets: 40in (1016mm) long x 5in (125mm) wide x 2in (50mm) deep
1 length of timber for poppet rests: 30in (762mm) long x 5in (125mm) wide x ¾in (19mm)
1 length of timber for the poppet keys: 24in (600mm) long x 3in (75mm) wide x 1in (25mm) deep
2 poles for the leg posts (I used chestnut): 66in (1676mm) long x 5in (125mm) diameter
4 poles for the braces: 36in (914mm) long x 3½in (89mm) diameter
1 length of timber for the tool rest:
2in (50mm) wide x 1½in (38mm) deep
1 pole for the pole: 216in (5486mm) long x 2-3in (50-75mm) diameter
2 poles for the pole supports: 36in (914mm) long x 2in (50mm) diameter
2 poles for the pole supports: 72in (1828mm) long x 2in (50mm) diameter
Threaded bar, washers and nuts: 30in (762mm) of 1in (25mm) diameter
6 screws: 1½in (38mm) (stainless if using oak or chestnut)
Threaded bar: 12in (300mm) long x ½in (12mm) diameter
Steel bar: 12in (300mm) long x ½in (12mm) diameter
3 nuts: ½in (12mm) diameter thread
Steel plate: 9in (228mm) x 1½in (38mm)
Paracord: 96in (2438mm) long x ⅛in (3mm) diameter

Recommended tools

Panel saw, Japanese saw, chisel, maul, twybil, draw knife, drill, auger bits 1in (25mm) and ⅝in (15mm), plane, impact driver, post rammer, sledgehammer, spirit level, clamps, string line, carpenter's square, welding equipment.

My first pole lathe was based on an early design of Mike Abbott's and is still serviceable after more than 20 years. For this project, I have gone for a similar design but with a traditional bed fixed in position in the woods using a long pole. I will, however, give dimensions for making the lathe transportable by creating a softwood triangulated frame for fixing the bed to and options for a spring conversion. I have made the bed from oak for longevity out in the woods.

Leg posts

Point the two 5in (125mm) diameter leg posts and, using the post rammer, hammer them firmly into the ground. The distance from the outside of one post to the outside of the other should be 60in (1524mm) ①. The height of the top of these posts will vary depending on your height and, in relation to your height, the working height you wish the bed to be at. I have set the height for the top of my bed – the posts will be 42in (1066mm) high out of the ground.

Brace the legs by fixing the angled support braces to the legs ②. These should be knocked into the ground with a sledgehammer at about 45 degrees and then offered across the legs, marked and sawn off, then pre-drilled and fixed with an impact driver and 6in (150mm) timber lock or coach screw. If setting your pole lathe up in the woods you could use two similar diameter coppice poles and cut them off at your chosen working height and fix the bed between them.

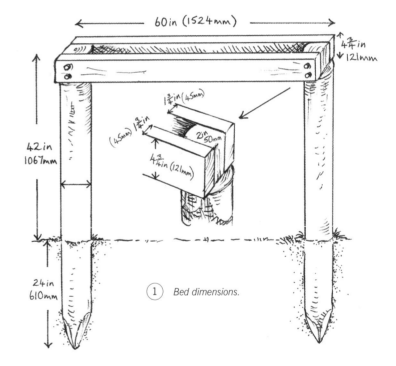

① Bed dimensions.

Braced legs.

Preparing the bed

With the help of another person, or by using two clamps to rest the bed plank on, offer one of the bed planks across the two poles with a spirit level on top and mark on each pole the top and bottom positions of the bed. Saw the top off each post and, using a string line stretched between the posts, mark two parallel lines on top of the posts 2in (50mm) apart.

Saw 2in (50mm) into each side of both posts where you have marked the position for the bottom of the bed and chisel down from the two parallel lines on top of the post to remove the waste and leave you with the centre 2in (50mm) of the post standing proud with a right-angled ledge each side, upon which the planks of the bed will sit ③. Check the bed planks are level in both directions and adjust the ledges if necessary ④.

Clamp the bed planks to the post and drill two 1in (25mm) holes through each end of the bed and secure the bed to the posts with the 1in (25mm) threaded bar, washers and nuts ⑤. I have reused some old studded bar, which, after some lubrication, has worked out fine. As my lathe will live outside with a cover over it, I have made sure to give it a good coat of linseed oil to help protect it.

ABOVE LEFT: Creating the right-angled ledge for the bed.

LEFT: Checking the bed is level in both planes.

BELOW: Completed bed.

Pole lathe history

The picture shows quite an advanced workshop with windows, shelves and tool racks. The early bodgers worked in a simple hovel with the roof and walls often made from the multitude of shavings that fall from the bodger's chisel.

Poppets

The poppets are designed to slide along the bed and are tightened by the tapered key under the bed, which can be hammered tight. Having two moveable poppets gives you a choice of position of where to work and allows you the full length of the bed for larger pieces.

First cut out the poppet shape from the 5 x 2in (125 x 50mm) using drawing ⑥. Then lay one section of the bed across the poppet blank at right angles to it and draw lines to mark the top and bottom of the bed on each poppet ⑦. Using a 1in (25mm) auger bit, drill three holes in the centre of the poppet, with the first hole overlapping above the line marking the position of the bottom of the bed by ½in (12mm), the second and third holes directly below the first.

Use the twybil to cut out the mortices ⑧ ⑨. Saw the poppet keys to size as in drawing ⑥ and curve off the tapered edge using a draw knife ⑩. Check that the key is a good fit into the poppet mortice and adjust if necessary ⑪.

Saw out the poppet rests and cut rebates into the poppets for the rests with a panel saw and chisel. These can be pre-drilled and fixed with screws (stainless steel screws if using oak or chestnut) ⑫.

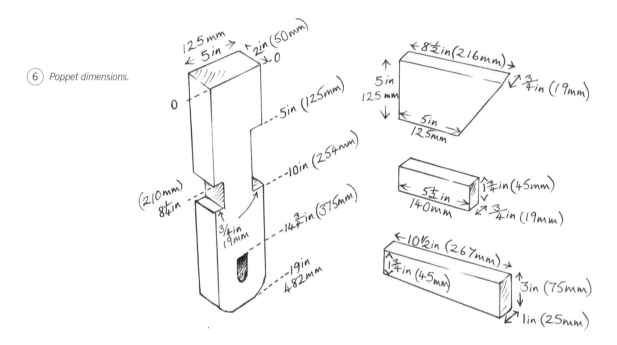

⑥ *Poppet dimensions.*

Laying the bed plank over the poppet to mark the top and bottom lines.

Using the twybil to cut the mortice edges.

The completed mortice.

Creating a curve on the tapered edge of the key with a draw knife.

Fitting the key to the poppet mortice.

Fixing the poppet rests to the poppets using stainless steel screws. Always pilot the hole prior to screwing through the wood with a drill bit slightly smaller than the diameter of the screw to avoid splitting the wood.

Alternative frame for a portable lathe

To make the portable 'A' frame you will need approximately 300in (7620mm) of 4 x 2in (100 x 50mm) of good-quality softwood. Douglas fir would be my preferred choice, and approximately 150in (3810mm) of 3 x 1½in (75mm x 38mm) for the horizontals.

The frame can be secured well by using timber locks but screws would also be fine. The 2in (50mm) width of the 4 x 2in (100 x 50mm) will create the space between

the bed planks for the poppets. I have shown the length to be 36in (914mm) but this can be shortened or extended depending upon your chosen working height. Make the 'A' frames up on a level surface and aim to have the diagonals at 45 degrees.

This design makes your pole lathe quite portable and easy to break down into components for transportation.

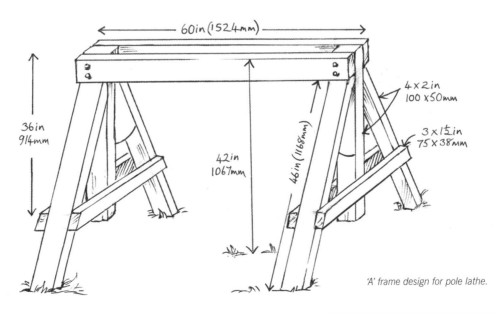

'A' frame design for pole lathe.

Fit the ironwork

The ironwork creates the two centre points that hold the wood centrally while the lathe is in operation. For this you will need to weld, or find a welder to weld three ½in (12mm) nuts to a strip of thin steel, each pre-drilled with a pair of screw holes, and create a crank handle from threaded bar and non-threaded steel bar (13)(14).

I had a set made up about 25 years ago. They have lived outside but with a good amount of lubrication they are still working and I have reused them for this lathe. As I am building an outside lathe, I have used oak and chestnut for durability. Oak and chestnut will corrode steel if they are in contact. I get around this by drilling a larger diameter hole through

the poppet than the diameter of the threaded bar, so that the handle is turning independently on the pair of welded nuts at each end of the poppet.

Drill a ⅝in (15mm) hole through the poppet 2in (50mm) from the top (15). Screw the steel plate with welded nuts to each side of the poppet over the hole you have drilled and wind the crank handle through. It should turn easily on the two nuts and should run parallel through the poppet. For the other poppet, a short piece of threaded bar can be welded to the nut as this centre point is fixed. Make sure that it lines up with the crank handle in the other poppet. The poppets can now be fitted to the bed using the wooden keys (16)(17).

(13)

Ironwork for the centre points.

(14) *Cranked handle dimensions.*

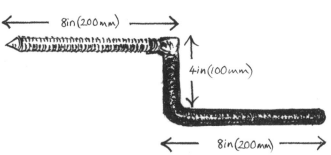

8in (200mm)

4in (100mm)

8in (200mm)

(15)

Drilling through the poppet for the cranked handle threaded bar.

(16)

Hammering in the key to secure the poppet to the bed.

(17)

Poppets set up on the bed.

Treadle

The treadle can be made from sawn wood – roofing baton works well but I prefer a traditional forked treadle with all the strength grown into the one piece of wood. My treadle is from chestnut but any forked piece of approximately 3in (75mm) diameter will work fine ⑱. The treadle needs to be attached to a footplate. This is a plank about 10in (250mm) wide and at least 24in (600mm) long.

The treadle is attached to the plank using 'T'-hinges. I chiselled a flat face onto each of the forked parts of the treadle branch ⑲ and screwed the 'T'-hinge into the treadle and then screwed the other part to the footplate ⑳. A cross brace is then fixed across the treadle. This will be where your foot moves up and down to turn the lathe, so the position of the cross brace will be a personal choice and you may try it in a few positions before deciding which one works best for you ㉑.

⑱ *Treadle dimensions.*

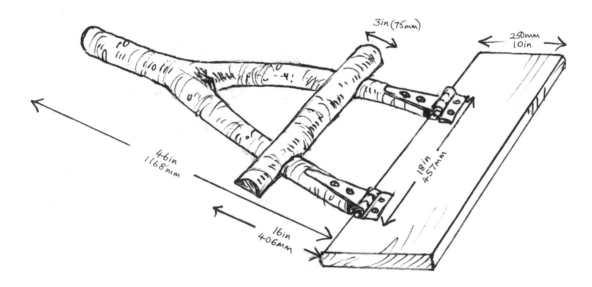

Chiselling the flats on the treadle for the 'T'-hinges.

A 'T'-hinge joining the treadle branch to the footplate.

Completed treadle.

Pole

This can be any wood that has a good amount of spring in it. I have used ash, birch and rowan but many other woods will suffice. The pole needs to be about 216in (5486mm) long and about 2–3in (50–75mm) diameter at the base tapering towards the tip. It will need supporting at the base and again further up. I hammered two 36in (914mm) long x 2in (50mm) diameter poles into the ground so they formed an 'X' shape. I lashed them together and then slid the base of the pole beneath them and lashed that to them.

The support that is further up the pole is of a similar construction but from 72in (1828mm) long poles. The position of this support will vary depending upon the thickness of the pole. Try it in one position and if the pole is not flexible enough, move the support further towards the base (22). Attach the cord from the end of the treadle to the end of your pole. The cord should wrap twice around your workpiece. Try the treadle and check the rotation is even. Lay a tool rest across the poppets so that it supports your chisel and brings it close to the workpiece. You are now ready to start turning (23) (24).

Setting up the pole: the support can be moved backwards or forwards to find the right amount of spring in the pole.

Ready to go: notice the tool rest across the poppets.

Lathe in action.

Adapting the lathe

Adapted spring lathe.

You may not have the space to set up your lathe with a long pole. Adapting it to a spring-style lathe saves space and, for me, creates a preferable lathe to the traditional pole style.

Attach two poles 72in (1828mm) long x 1½in (38mm) diameter, one to each side of the frame. Stretch a bicycle inner tube across the two poles so that it sits above the bed of the lathe. Attach your cord from the inner tube to the treadle and wrap twice around your workpiece as usual.

Traditional spring lathe.

STEAMER

Steam bending involves saturating the fibres of wood and then bending them. I liken steam bending to cooking spaghetti. It is hard when raw and when you bend it, it snaps. After cooking, it becomes pliable and then once it has cooled down it begins to harden again. Steam bending wood follows the same pattern except the wood sets to a more solid form and partially seasons through the process.

Materials you will need

This project involves using a 45-gallon (204-litre) drum and a marine-ply steam box. The size of the box can be varied to adapt to the design of project you are making.

1 oil drum or similar: 45 gallons (204 litres)
1 sheet of marine ply: 96in (2438mm) long x 48in (1219mm) wide x 1in (25mm) deep
20 bricks
1 box stainless steel screws: 1½in (38mm)
2 small hinges
hook and eye

Recommended tools

Jigsaw, screwdriver, angle grinder, drill, 1½in (38mm) auger bit or bar auger.

Example of a steamer using an army field kitchen and steel box steamer for making yurt hoops.

Create a steamer

First build a dry brick wall to support the oil drum. Leave gaps between the bricks for air flow and an entrance for adding wood. The dry brick wall must be stable enough to support the oil drum full of water. Cut a slot in the top of the oil drum 2in (50mm) wide x 12in (300mm) long. Cut a square section out of the marine ply sheet 26 x 26in (660 x 660mm). Using the jigsaw cut out a 2in (50mm) wide x 12in (300mm) long slot in the square section and lay on top of the oil drum with the slots overlapping ①.

Slot cut into square piece of ply over the oil drum.

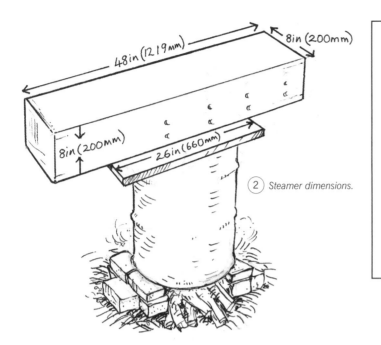

48in (1219mm)

8in (200mm)

8in (200mm)

26in (660mm)

(2) *Steamer dimensions.*

Steam bending

To steam bend wood you need a steamer to create the steam and a steam box into which you insert the wood that is being steamed. To create the steam you need heat and a vessel of water. This can be an electric wallpaper stripper for small projects through to an industrial water boiler for larger projects. You will also need 'bending forms' (see page 195), which are shaped objects with which you clamp the steam-bent wood to get it to set to your desired shape.

(3)

Using the bar auger to drill out holes in the base of the rectangular box.

Distributing the steam

Drill ½in (12mm) holes through the sides of the steam box and fix dowels across the box to support workpieces. This allows a good distribution of steam around multiple workpieces.

Steam box with dowels to support multiple workpieces.

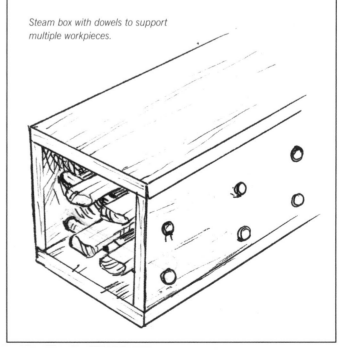

Cut out four 8in (200mm) x 48in (1219mm) strips of marine ply and screw them together to make a rectangular ply box (2). Cut out two end pieces and screw one end on the box. On the other end, fix hinges and hook and eye to make a door. Drill out a number of 1½in (38mm) holes in the bottom of the box so that they lay over the slot in the square piece of ply (3). Screw the box and square piece of ply together.

Light a fire under the oil drum and, once boiling, steam will work its way into the steam box and saturate the fibres of the workpiece. Laying old carpet over the box can help insulate the steamer and slow down the escape of steam.

Completed steamer in use.

Ladder-back slats in a vice bending form.

Bending forms

The steamer creates the ability to steam your timber so that you can bend it. The bending forms are designed to secure the timber in place, so that it sets to your desired shape. Bending forms vary in size and materials, depending upon the thickness of the workpiece you are bending. At an extreme, I have used a timber-framed construction fixed to trees to bend 5in (125mm) diameter roundwood rafters. More delicate bending forms involve bending chair legs and ladder-back slats.

Chair leg bending form.

Yurt hoop bending form.

Glossary

Adze
An axe-like tool with its blade at right angles to its handle, used to shape and dress timber.

'A' frame
A truss formed by two main timbers with a tie beam, making a join resembling the letter 'A'.

Auger
A hand drill, for boring holes in wood.

Billet
A small chunk of wood, often in the process of being made into a final product.

Selection of bar and Scotch-eyed augers.

Blank (for a spoon).

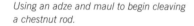

Using an adze and maul to begin cleaving a chestnut rod.

Billhook
A traditional hand tool made in many different patterns. It has a wooden handle and usually a curved blade used for cutting and snedding coppice.

Bevel
An angled sloping edge.

Blank
A piece of wood that is prepared for a specific craft purpose but is unfinished.

Bodger
The name for craftsmen who make chair legs on a pole lathe.

Box frame
A term used to describe a form of construction where the building is framed out of horizontal and vertical timbers to produce a wooden box.

Brake
A device used for holding a piece of wood while being cleaved into smaller sections.

Brash
Small branches from the side and top of trees.

A shake brake.

Butterpat joint.

Bundler.

Cleaving with a froe.

Butterpat joint
A scribed joint that resembles a pat of butter in a dish, often where the cruck meets the tie-beam on a roundwood timber frame.

Bundler
A device for holding woodland produce to help enable the tying of a bundle.

Cant
A defined area of coppice, also regionally referred to as a 'panel'.

Cleave
To split unsawn timber by forcing the fibres apart along its length.

Coach screw
A large, heavy-duty screw with a square head often used with larger timbers.

Collett
A band put around a shaft and tightened in order to grip it.

Compound angle
A compound angle is formed by cutting a piece of wood at an angle to both its horizontal and vertical planes.

Coppice
Broadleaf trees cut during the dormant season, which produce multi-stems that are harvested for wood products.

Dovetail joint
A flaring tenon and a mortice into which it fits tightly, making an interlocking joint between two pieces, which resists pulling apart in all directions except one.

Dowel
A peg often used for holding together parts of a structure.

Draw knife
A sharp blade with a bevelled edge and two wooden handles used for shaving wood to a smaller size.

Re-emerging chestnut coppice at Prickly Nut Wood.

Shaving with a draw knife.

Faggots.

Framing bed.

Froe.

Faggot
A tied bundle of small branches traditionally used to fire ovens, now used for riverbank restoration and coastal defence.

Felling levers
A forestry device used when felling trees, often with a small cant hook attached for turning trees or logs.

Framing bed
A level platform made from strong timber bearers upon which timber frames can be jointed accurately.

Froe
A metal blade with a long handle used for cleaving wood into smaller sections.

Gate hurdle
A portable, lightweight hurdle, usually made from sweet chestnut or ash, which is traditionally used for penning or folding sheep.

Greenwood
Freshly cut, unseasoned wood.

Jig
A device that holds a piece of wood and guides the tool operating upon it.

Knee vice
A vice that holds wood to be peeled and is controlled by exerting pressure using the operator's knee.

Lath
Thin cleft strips of wood used primarily for a framework in a wall upon which plaster (traditionally lime) is applied.

Lathe
A device for shaping wood, which turns the piece of wood being worked on against the craftperson's chisel.

Two applewood mauls.

Woven chestnut laths with plaster being applied.

Lathe.

Mortice.

Bundles of chestnut pales in the background and some completed rolls of fencing in the foreground.

Lever post
A post in some designs of shaving horse that transfers the pressure from the operator's foot to the piece of work being held in position.

Maul
A handmade wooden mallet usually made from a tree branch.

Mortice
A chiselled slot into, or through, which a tenon is inserted.

Pale
A cleft section of chestnut heartwood usually wired to others to form a fence.

Pivot peg
A peg upon which a frame can pivot, which is used in the construction of shaving horses.

Poppet
Adjustable grip that can be moved along the bed of a pole lathe to allow different length pieces of wood to be turned.

Post rammer
A metal tube with handles on each side that can be slid over a wooden post to help ram it into the ground.

Rive
See cleave.

Roundwood timber framing
A timber-framing technique that uses round poles, as opposed to square wood, to construct buildings.

Constructing a roundwood timber-frame building.

A post rammer.

Sapwood
The soft outer layers of recently formed wood between the heartwood and the bark, containing the functioning vascular tissue.

Shackle
A metal link, typically 'U'-shaped, closed by a bolt, used to secure a chain or rope to something.

Shake
A cleft wooden roofing tile.

Shaving horse
A vice that clamps wood for the operator to peel in a seated position.

Shingle
A sawn wooden roofing tile.

Sliding bevel
An adjustable gauge for setting and transferring angles.

Using a froe to cleave a shake from a piece of oak.

Using a sliding bevel to transfer an angle of 65°.

Fitting red cedar roof shingles.

Snedding
Removal of side branches and top of a felled tree.

Spar
A (usually) twisted hazel staple used for securing thatch.

Strop
A piece of leather used for finishing the sharpening process of an edge tool.

Stool
The stump of a coppiced tree from which new stems grow; also a simple seat.

Tenon
The projecting end of a timber that is inserted into a mortice.

Threaded bar
Steel bar with a thread cut into it so that it can receive nuts to make a bolt of your chosen length.

Timber lock
A heavy duty screw fixing.

Timber tongs
A hand tool for gripping lengths of round timber to facilitate lifting or dragging the timber.

Spars.

Tenon.

Holding the workpiece in the top jaw.

Top jaw
The part of a shaving horse that holds the workpiece in place against the platform.

Treadle
A lever worked by the foot and imparting motion to a device or machine.

Wedge
A small angled piece of wood.

Winch
A winch is a mechanical device used to pull in (wind up), let out (wind out) or otherwise adjust the tension of a rope or wire rope.

Yurt
A wooden-framed transportable dwelling with canvas covering, originating from Asia and now found more regularly as a dwelling in woodlands.

A note on measurements

The measurements in this book are in both imperial and metric. Most craftsmen I know have a selection of drill bits, some metric and some imperial – this of course creates variations in degrees of measurement, which can be useful in precise work but also can be confusing at times. It is good practice to keep them separate.

Resources

Further reading

Ancient Woodland: Its History, Vegetation and Uses in England by Oliver Rackham (Castlepoint Press, 2003). The definitive text on ancient woodland.

Antiquaries Journal, volume LXVII, Part 1 (The Oxford University Press, 1987). Article on Iron Age and Roman Quern production at Lodsworth, West Sussex.

Carving and Whittling: The Swedish Style by Gert Ljungberg and Inger Ason Ljungberg (Lark Books, 1999).

Collins Guide To Tree Planting & Cultivation by Herbert L. Edlin (Collins; 1975). Recommended guide.

Complete Practical Book of Country Crafts by Jack Hill (David & Charles, 1979).

Coppicing and Coppice Crafts by Rebecca Oaks and Edward Mills (The Crowood Press, 2010). Good introduction to coppicing and crafts with Cumbrian flavour.

Country Craft Tools by Percy W. Blandford (Swan Hill Press, 1997).

Flora Brittanica by Richard Mabey (Chatto & Windus, 1996). The evolving culture of Britain's flora.

Going with the Grain: Making Chairs in the 21st Century by Mike Abbott (Living Woods Books, 2011). Detailed chair-making book from tree to finished product from one of the country's most experienced chair-making tutors.

Greenwood Crafts: A Comprehensive Guide by Edward Mills and Rebecca Oaks (The Crowood Press, 2012). Excellent complement to their coppicing and coppice crafts book.

Green Woodwork: Working with Wood the Natural Way by Mike Abbott (Guild of Master Craftsmen Publications, 1989).

Green Woodworking: A Hands-on Approach by Drew Langster (Lark Books, 1995).

Green Woodworker's Pattern Book by Ray Tabor (Batsford, 2005). An excellent, well-researched pattern book with many craft designs.

Living Wood: From Buying a Woodland to Making a Chair by Mike Abbott (Living Wood Books, 2013). Mike's journey of working in the wood with practical craftwork.

Make a Chair from a Tree: An Introduction to Working Green Wood by John D. Alexander, Jr (The Astragel Press, 1994).

Making Rustic Furniture by Daniel Mack (Lark Books, 1990). Inspirational.

Oak-Framed Buildings by Rupert Newman (Guild of Master Craftsman Publications, 2005, revised 2014).

Roundwood Timber Framing by Ben Law (Permanent Publications, 2016). A 'how-to' build with roundwood book.

Sharpening: the Complete Guide by Jim Kingshott (Guild of Master Craftsman Publications, 1991).

Shaving Horses, Lap Shaves and Other Woodland Vices by Sean Hellman (Crafty Little Press, 2017). A must for all shave horse lovers.

The Chairmaker's Workshop: Handcrafting Windsor and Post-and-Rung Chairs by Drew Langster (Lark Books, 1997).

The History of the Countryside by Oliver Rackham (W&N, 2000). A fascinating description of how the British landscape and human activities have interacted over many centuries to create what we see today.

The New Sylva: A Discourse of Forest and Orchard Trees for the Twenty-First Century by Gabriel Hemery and Sarah Simblet (Bloomsbury Publishing, 2014). Beautifully illustrated update on John Evelyn's original work.

The Rustic Furniture Companion: Traditions, Techniques and Inspirations by Daniel Mack (Lark Books, 1996).

Further inspiration

The Woodland House by Ben Law (Permanent Publications, 2013). Building a roundwood sweet chestnut house in a woodland.

The Woodland Way: A Permaculture Approach to Sustainable Woodland by Ben Law (Permanent Publications, 2001, revised in 2015). A classic text on sustainable woodland management.

The Woodland Year by Ben Law (Permanent Publications, 2008). My month-by-month guide to working the woods and producing associated crafts, including entries from other woodland craftsmen.

The Woodwright's Shop by Roy Underhill (The University of North Carolina Press, 1981).

Tools and Devices For Coppice Crafts by F. Lambert (Centre for Alternative Technology; first published as a Young Farmers' Club booklet, 1957). Hard to read, but many useful designs.

Traditional Country Craftsmen by J. Geraint Jenkins (Routledge and Kegan Paul, 1965).

Traditional Woodland Crafts by Raymond Tabor (Batsford, 1994) Well illustrated and practical.

Trees and Woodland in the British Landscape: The Complete History of Britain's Trees, Woods and Hedgerows by Oliver Rackham (Weidenfeld & Nicolson, 1995). Excellent historical perspective.

Woodland Craft by Ben Law (Guild of Master Craftsman Publications, 2015). Step-by-step instructions to making woodland crafts, old and new.

Woodland Crafts in Britain by Herbert L. Edlin (David & Charles, 1949). A classic text, now out of print.

Woodsman: Living in a Wood in the 21st Century by Ben Law (Collins, 2014). My journey to becoming a woodsman.

Tool suppliers

Ashley Iles (Edge Tools) Ltd
www.ashleyiles.co.uk
Edge tools including twybil

Axminster Tools
www.axminster.co.uk
Japanese water stones, diamond stones, grinding wheels

Bristol Design
www.bristol-design.co.uk
Froes

Fraught Wrought, Michael Stanton
fraughtwrought@btinternet.com

Old Tool Store
www.oldtoolstore.com
Secondhand tools

Quercus
www.quirkyquercus.co.uk
Froes and twybils

The Woodsmiths Experience
www.woodsmithexperience.co.uk
Good range of Green woodworking tools

Thomas Flinn and Co
www.flinn-garlick-saws.co.uk
Traditional handsaws, saw setting tools and two-person crosscut saws

Timber Framing Tools
www.tftools.co.uk
Timber framing chisels, WoodOwl auger bits

Timeless Tools
www.timelesstools.co.uk
Secondhand edge tools

Woodland Craft Supplies
www.woodlandcraftsupplies.co.uk
Green woodworking tools

Workshop Stoves
www.workshopstoves.co.uk
Wood and sawdust burning stoves for the workshop

About the author

Ben Law, woodsman, craftsman, eco-builder, teacher and writer, lives and works in Prickly Nut Wood in West Sussex, UK. The building of his unique woodland home was featured on Channel 4's *Grand Designs* in the UK and was voted by viewers as the most popular episode ever. In addition to the coppicing of his own woodland, he runs courses on sustainable woodland management and permaculture and trains apprentices. Ben Law is the author of several books, including *The Woodland House* (Permanent Publications, 2005), *The Woodland Year* (Permanent Publications, 2008), *Woodsman: Living in a Wood in the 21st Century* (HarperCollins, 2013) and *Woodland Craft* (GMC Publications, 2015).
www.ben-law.co.uk

Acknowledgements

I must thank my overwhelming inspiration, Prickly Nut Wood in West Sussex, my teacher for more than twenty-five years. I would like to thank Will Hannam and Vikki Mill who apprenticed with me over the past couple of years and helped on many projects and with the management of the coppice woods. A special thanks to Claire Soper for her love and friendship and to my brother Dan for taking the deer management in the woods to the next level. A thank you to my two lurchers, Barley and Pirate, for their excellent squirrel management and to my children Rowan (now graduated in shake making!), Zed and Tess for the joy they bring to woodland life.

Index

Picture credits

All photographs by Ben Law except:

Andrew Perris: pages 2, 3, 4, 5, 9, 10, 11 (all, except top right), 22, 23, 27, 28, 31, 32, 35, 38, 39 (top right), 40, 45, 48, 51 (top right), 55, 56, 60, 63, 75, 82, 83, 85, 93, 107, 115 (bottom right), 130, 131, 135, 136, 137, 150, 151, 155, 161, 170,171, 196 (bottom left and bottom right), 197 (all, except top right), 201 (top left), 204 (left) and 208.
John Topham/TopFoto.co.uk: page 71.
TopFoto.co.uk: pages 117 and 183.
West Sussex Record Office: pages 76 and 177.
Rebecca Mothersole: page 81 (bottom right) and 204 (bottom right).

To order a book, or to request
a catalogue, contact:
GMC Publications Ltd, Castle Place,
166 High Street, Lewes, East Sussex
BN7 1XU, United Kingdom
Tel: +44 (0)1273 488005
www.gmcbooks.com